HIDDEN HEROES

Transforming
an Ordinary Life *into*
an EXTRAORDINARY
ADVENTURE

Larry Thompson

xulon
PRESS

Copyright © 2005 by Larry Thompson

Hidden Heroes
by Larry Thompson

Printed in the United States of America

ISBN 1-59781-290-0

All rights reserved solely by the author. No part of this book may be reproduced in any form without the permission of the author.

Unless otherwise indicated, Scripture is taken from the HOLY BIBLE, NEW INTERNATIONAL VERSION®. NIV®. Copyright © 1973, 1978, 1984 by International Bible Society. Used by permission of Zondervan. All rights reserved.

As often as possible, we've provided resources, permissions and citations for stories we've told and heroes we've written about. We hope we've included everyone appropriately. If not, please accept our apology in advance and let us know. Any corrections may be included in future editions.

www.HiddenHeroesBook.com

www.xulonpress.com

Table of Contents

Introduction xi
Chapter 1: Shaphan: Ancient Words 15
Chapter 2: Jubal: An Instrument of Praise 29
Chapter 3: Jehosheba: The Messianic Bloodline 45
Chapter 4: Joab: Leadership Essential 55
Chapter 5: Huldah: Woman of Influence 69
Chapter 6: Mephibosheth: Transformed by Grace 77
Chapter 7: Ebed-Melech: Servant of the King 89
Chapter 8: Araunah: When Little Becomes Much 99
Chapter 9: Bezaleel: Gifted Child of God 113
Chapter 10: Eunice: Mother with a Mission 127
Chapter 11: Anna: Super Senior Saint 137
Chapter 12: Simon of Cyrene: Divine Interruption 149
Chapter 13: CSI Jerusalem: Mystery Solved 159
Chapter 14: Déjà You: Joy Restored 167
Conclusion 177

Foreword

When the final accounting is done one day, we will learn that God's "hidden heroes" on earth far outnumbered the famous men and women whose names are more easily recognizable. Of course, the fact that some are briefly mentioned in the Bible reminds us that God affirmed their unique contribution to His kingdom. Though not entirely unsung, they moved on a different and smaller stage than that of those Biblical characters like King David and the Apostle Paul.

My friend Larry Thompson has written this book to inspire faith in God for the common places of life, away from the spotlight that brings recognition and applause. Each day, he works among hidden heroes who serve his community. You'll read about some of them in this book. Many more will remain unknown to us, but will be highly honored by the One who matters most. As you read these words, ask yourself, "Who are the unseen heroes in my life, in my community?" By taking a closer look at the heroes hidden within the pages of the Bible, we can discover more about the heroes hidden in our everyday lives. I think you'll also find that there's the potential for a heroic spiritual life, ready to rise forth from your own heart. We certainly can't all achieve notoriety on earth, but as we daily follow Jesus we can join God's legion of Hidden Heroes.

Jim Cymbala
The Brooklyn Tabernacle
New York, New York

Acknowledgments

I have always said I wouldn't write a book just to write a book...I promised myself and the Lord I would not write a book unless I knew there was leadership from Him and there was something that needed to be said in way that could encourage and inspire others...so if you find "Hidden Heroes" encouraging, inspirational, or challenging then pause with me to thank God, the One who is constantly transforming an ordinary life into an extra-ordinary adventure!

To the three most important girls in my life: Cynthia, Ami Taylor and Jennifer. Some people go their entire lives failing to meet or see a real life "Hidden Hero" in action. Yet I have had the privilege of living with three of them every day! I love you so much and I thank you for making my life so full, rich and wonderful.

As I reflect on the blessings of my family, I thank the Lord and Jennifer for bringing Mason into our lives. Mason, thank you for being a man with a heart for God.

One truth I have learned about a "Hidden Hero"...the accomplishments of his or her life would be impossible without a team of people who believed in the vision and had the courage to act when the spotlight of opportunity was focused on them. I am blessed to work and serve with an outstanding ministry team of men and women which understands the urgency of the moment and the realization of this truth: "Hidden Heroes," all working together under His power, can accomplish anything for His glory!

A special word of thanks to *Mike Jeffries*, my friend, fellow servant, and my armor-bearer. Your tireless effort in seeing this project through to completion brought peace and great joy to my work.

Many of the characters in this book were first discovered as our church pursued a search of the Bible's unheralded heroes during our Sunday-morning Worship Celebrations. Each week, hundreds of children joined me in that search, drawing from clues we had given them the week before. I'm so proud of our children, and proud of their pursuit of God's Word.

After more than thirty years in professional ministry I am overwhelmed as I consider all the "Hidden Heroes" who have impacted my life and influenced this book. I feel so great an indebtedness to each of them and especially to each church the Lord gave me the honor of serving.

Finally, my heartfelt love and thanks to the greatest people on the face of the earth, *the members of First Baptist Church of Fort Lauderdale*. You have taught me so much through the years and I humbly thank you for the privilege of serving you and loving you as together we see the reality of His vision fulfilled in our presence; a vision to be a biblically based, global community of believers, glorifying Jesus Christ by building radical relationships for life!

Introduction

Noah, Abraham, Joseph, Moses, Rahab, Joshua, David, Samson, Mary, Paul, Peter, John…of course you know them. Actually, you have heard about them your entire life. The Bible refers to them as heroes. They are our champions; they stood the test of time and stood with God. Because of their faith, the Bible tells us, they are tremendous examples for all of us today. They were not perfect; they had their problems and trials, and even dealt with personal sin. Yet in their obedience to God they were ready to serve when the Father called their names. Yes, absolutely, you know their names—and indeed, they were real heroes of the faith!

What about Shaphan, Huldah, Araunah, and Bezaleel… ever heard of them? Probably not. Yet they, along with many more people, have something in common with our list of well known biblical heroes: They too have earned the right to the title of hero, even if they happen to be Hidden Heroes. Each of these individuals appears in only a verse or two of Scripture, and yet each played a vitally significant role in shaping our spiritual future. They have been ignored by scholars, commentators, and pastors; as a result, we have failed to provide people with a wonderful opportunity to both be inspired by and identify with these Hidden Heroes.

The Bible is a wonderful reflection of life, in every time in history. As in the biblical world, our world is filled with our own selection of spiritual heroes. After all, who wouldn't want to serve in an army where Billy Graham was leading the charge for righteousness? What an honor it would be to sit at the feet of Dr. Bill Bright and have him share his vision for world evangelism! Can you imagine being invited to the most impoverished area of India to meet Mother Teresa and watch her as she touched the untouchables with the love of Jesus Christ? The names of our modern-day heroes are as honored as the biblical heroes of the faith. Have you ever stopped to consider that we also have a world full of modern-day Hidden Heroes?

I have said for more than thirty years that I would not write a book just to write a book. I have always maintained that if the Lord ever allowed me to write, it would be because He had given me something that could encourage people and provide inspiration from a fountain of fresh thought.

My personal journey through God's Word began several years ago when, at a time of great need in my own life, I made a vow to God that I would never begin another day without first opening the Bible to seek His truth and direction for the day ahead. I have honored that vow and, in all honesty, it no longer feels like a vow to me but an absolute necessity. It has been the key to what God has done in the development of my spiritual maturity. As a result of that vow, I noticed year after year that I was being introduced to the "minor" characters of the Bible. Each year through the Bible, I would pause and again reflect on the wonderful impact they made when given their "fifteen minutes of fame." After personally enjoying and being challenged by these unknowns of Scripture, I decided that I would develop a series that would highlight the individuals and their personal contributions to our faith.

An amazing truth began to develop as I prepared these messages and this book, a truth so simple that it is easily missed and forgotten. If the Bible has so many Hidden

Introduction

Heroes, shouldn't we be challenged to look for that one opportunity to transform an ordinary life into an extraordinary adventure?

Without a doubt, I believe each person who reads this book has the potential to be a Hidden Hero. Many of you are already qualified to wear that designation proudly. My goal for sharing this concept with you is not simply to acquaint you with some wonderful men and women of Scripture but also to light a fire within your heart. Please listen for His call. We have plenty of heroes in our society. What we need is one more Hidden Hero. Personally, I think you fit the description perfectly! Enjoy the adventure.

Larry L. Thompson
Fort Lauderdale, Florida

CHAPTER 1

Shaphan: Ancient Words

Indiana Jones and the Lost Ark. Howard Carter and the tomb of King Tutankhamun. Christopher Columbus and the New World. Shrek and Princess Fiona. Albert Einstein and the theory of relativity. Pierre Francois-Bouchard and the Rosetta Stone. Ferdinand Magellan and the "peaceful sea," the Pacific Ocean. Thomas Edison and the light bulb. The crew of the Starship Enterprise and "where no man has gone before." All of these....amazing discoveries. Some of them are real. Some are imagined. And some are somewhere in between. But one of the greatest real-life discoveries in the last hundred years stands with them all.

Shortly after World War II and just before Israel became a nation again, a Bedouin shepherd boy was searching for his lost goat. He threw a rock into a cave in Qumran, about thirteen miles east of Jerusalem, hoping to prod the goat from its mountainous hiding place. The rock hit something, but it wasn't a goat. The Bedouin boy and his fellow shepherds explored the cave further and found one of the greatest archaeological discoveries of all time. For nearly two thousand years, what we now know as the Dead Sea Scrolls had been hidden from robber and raider, undisturbed and waiting for their debut in modernity.

A few years ago, my wife and I visited a museum called the Shrine of the Book in Israel's capital city and saw these texts up close. The significance of these scrolls? The Dead Sea Scrolls, discovered on a lazy afternoon by a few itinerant shepherds, represent the most important Bible discovery of modern times. Within these caves at Qumran, archaeologists have found more than fifteen thousand fragments of ancient biblical and nonbiblical writings, more than five hundred manuscripts, and about 850 different scrolls. According to the Dead Sea scholars, the find included at least a portion of every book from the Old Testament, except for one. They found nineteen copies of Isaiah, twenty-five copies of Deuteronomy, and thirty copies of the Psalms. Written in Hebrew and Aramaic, the scrolls and text fragments were made of papyrus, parchment, leather, and copper.

One of the scrolls, called the Temple Scroll, is nearly twenty-seven feet long. The Isaiah scroll, one of the more complete of those found, is at least a millennium older than any other known copy of Isaiah. Indeed, every Old Testament portion represents the oldest of its kind ever found. When the Dead Sea Scrolls discovery was made public, newspapers conjectured about the mysteries held within, and scholars wondered how thousands of years of study would be changed. Fear, excitement, amazement, confusion....during the wonder years of the middle twentieth century, these were all emotions associated with the discovery of these ancient scrolls in the Judean desert.

Now imagine a similar scene, nearly three thousand years earlier, in the middle of the ninth century B.C. The people of God had been given five books of law and history through the ministry and administration of Moses. Other leaders followed, the people of Israel moved into the Promised Land, and kings were established the rule this new state. Saul, David, and Solomon ruled with varying results over a united kingdom, a chosen nation. During the reign of Solomon's son Rehoboam, ten of the tribes of Israel decided to start their own nation, what became known as the northern kingdom. Rehoboam ruled the southern kingdom, Judah, and the northern kingdom of Israel began its own line of royal succession.

For centuries, faithful followers had relied on the Word of God to guide their daily lives and the workings of their communities and nation. Now, with kingdoms divided, it became obvious why God warned His chosen people against rallying for an earthly king. Though they were far from perfect, the first few kings of Judah were still faithful in many ways. (Not so in the northern kingdom of Israel, where rebellion led to evil reigns almost immediately.) But Jehoshaphat was the last of these good kings before several evil kings began their wicked reigns of oppression and idolatry.

Inconsistency marked the next several kings. Some were okay. Some were among the most evil. During this time, not only was the Word of God ignored, it was literally lost. The sacred scrolls that had so strongly guided the people of Israel were hidden, scattered, misplaced, or destroyed.

Within the records of 2 Kings is an amazing story about a man who was secretary to a young king. God used his openness and his opportunity to impact not only a family but also an entire nation. As you study the kings of the Old Testament, you'll have a hard time finding one truly committed to following God completely. David was one, although even he had his well-known difficulties. Another one was Josiah. Josiah began his reign at the age of eight, following his father's short two-year reign and his grandfather's enduring but inconsistent fifty-five-year reign. The biblical record tells us that Josiah "did what was right in the eyes of the Lord and walked in all the ways of his father David, not turning aside to the right or to the left." When he was only twenty-six years old, Josiah pronounced his intention to restore the temple, which represented the spiritual home of his people. A person's major work for God may have to wait until he is an adult, but no one is ever too young to take God seriously. Josiah's early years became the basis for his later task of reforming Judah.

While the emergence of an eight-year-old king is certainly intriguing, even more intriguing is the court behind the king. What was the foundation in this young boy's life that allowed him to become one of the greatest kings in the history of Israel? The answer becomes apparent when you find the Hidden Hero in 2 Kings 22:

> Josiah was eight years old when he became king, and he reigned in Jerusalem thirty-one years. His mother's name was Jedidah daughter of Adaiah. She was from Bozkath. He did what was right in the eyes of the Lord and walked in all the ways of his father David, not turning aside to the right or to the left.
>
> In the eighteenth year of his reign, King Josiah sent the secretary, Shaphan son of Azaliah, the son of Meshullam, to the temple of the LORD. He said: "Go up to Hilkiah the high priest and have him get ready the money that has been brought into the temple of the LORD, which the doorkeepers have collected from the people. Have them entrust it to the men appointed to supervise the work on the temple. And have these men pay the workers who repair the temple of the LORD—the carpenters, the builders and the masons. Also have them purchase timber and dressed stone to repair the temple. But they need not account for the money entrusted to them, because they are acting faithfully."
>
> Hilkiah the high priest said to Shaphan the secretary, "I have found the Book of the Law in the temple of the LORD." He gave it to Shaphan, who read it. Then Shaphan the secretary went to the king and reported to him: "Your officials have paid out the money that was in the temple of the LORD and have

entrusted it to the workers and supervisors at the temple." Then Shaphan the secretary informed the king, "Hilkiah the priest has given me a book." And Shaphan read from it in the presence of the king.

When the king heard the words of the Book of the Law, he tore his robes. He gave these orders to Hilkiah the priest, Ahikam son of Shaphan, Acbor son of Micaiah, Shaphan the secretary and Asaiah the king"s attendant: "Go and inquire of the LORD for me and for the people and for all Judah about what is written in this book that has been found. Great is the LORD's anger that burns against us because our fathers have not obeyed the words of this book; they have not acted in accordance with all that is written there concerning us" (verses 1–13).

Within these thirteen verses are several observations about the life of Shaphan that reveal the importance of God's Word and the reason this Hidden Hero had such an impact in the history of Israel. Not only did Shaphan make a defining discovery, but also his days as a disciple of God allowed him to be an essential part of a divine destiny.

Try to put yourself in this scene. The temple had been in disrepair, with the destruction coming more from the spiritual apathy and atrophy of God's people than from overuse or conquering armies. King Josiah was spiritually aware enough to rebuild the temple in hopes that the hearts of men and women will be rebuilt as well. One day, the king was doing some accounting and construction planning, so he entrusted his secretary with an important errand.

Shaphan traveled to the temple, disbursed money to the workers, and began a conversation with the high priest overseeing the reconstruction. "I have found the Book of the Law in the temple of the Lord," said the high priest. Shaphan knew this had to be reported to the king immediately. We don't know all the details about the discovery. But judging by the reaction of the king, it seems as though the Book of the Law had been lost for some time. Perhaps as a young boy, the king had heard priests and elders talking about the words of Moses and how they lamented their loss.

Imagine never having an opportunity to see a copy of the Declaration of Independence or the Constitution. Maybe you read about it in another book or heard some of your teachers talking about it. Now imagine never having held a Bible in your own hands. Your parents may have talked about some of the stories in the Bible. But you'd never actually held one. Unimaginable? It was reality for King Josiah; even the king couldn't get his hands on the Bible of his time. So think of his joy, his wonder, his amazement, when his secretary walked in during an otherwise ordinary day and said, "The priest has given me a book." Talk about an understatement!

Shaphan knew that this was the Book of Books, the very words God had given to Moses. As a disciple of the Lord, disciplined in His ways, Shaphan opened the book that had been found and began reading to Josiah. Look at the illustration of Shaphan and the time in which he was living. The nation and the people had wandered from the truth of God's Word and the direction He had provided the people. The people in the days of Shaphan acted like many of the people in our culture today. They ignored the truth of God and traveled into the downward paths of their own devising!

For us, it will undoubtedly take a new and deep study of Scripture, which the Spirit will use as a means of recalling individuals, churches, and nations to the truth and will of God for our lives. When faced with the crisis of the day what will you do? If you are not committed to the Word and allowing God to use His Word in your life, you will simply resort to doing what you think is best, based on man's wisdom, man's strength, man's way. However, if you are following the example of this Hidden Hero as a true disciple, devoted to the truth of God's Word, then you may have the wisdom you need from God for the very moment you face the test. Shaphan is a Hidden Hero because he, like the other great giants of the faith whose influence has shaped the course of Christian history, derived his spiritual motivation from a renewed contact and obedience with the written Word.

King Josiah's story is well-known. But what about the secretary who rushed back to the palace to not only tell the king of this discovery but also to read the book to the king word for word? Shaphan personally acknowledged the importance of the Word of God in his life and was bold enough to share the Word of God with others. This is the picture of how God uses each of us to become Hidden Heroes when He honors our commitment to reading the Word of God and then sharing the Word with those we love. Shaphan could have said, "I have carried out your requests!" However, because Shaphan knew God's precepts, he was now compelled to share the written word with others. All you need to do is read on and see the incredible difference this obedience brings to the life of this man, his family, his king, and his nation.

The impact this had on Shaphan's family is especially significant. Look at how Shaphan's love for God's Word and obedience to the Word of God translated into a legacy for future generations. You have no idea what legacy God is giving you and preparing in the lives of your children, your friends, your family, and your co-workers simply because you care enough to daily spend time in the Word of God. In our Hidden Hero's life, we find the impact lasted well beyond the time in which he lived. His legacy impacted his children, and they had an impact on the Kingdom of God. Consider the progeny of Shaphan's promise:

Ahikam, son of Shaphan

In Jeremiah 26, King Jehoiakim ordered the death of men and women who prophesied the truth of the Lord, because it was a message the king did not want to hear. As the king was about to sentence Jeremiah to death, we find one of Shaphan's sons coming to the rescue. "Furthermore, Ahikam son of Shaphan supported Jeremiah, and so he was not handed over to the people to be put to death" (Jer. 26:24). Why did Ahikam stand up for Jeremiah? Because this son had been reared with truth and was bold enough to stand in obedience to the truth!

Elasah, son of Shaphan

Now look at this next verse: "He [Jeremiah] entrusted the letter to Elasah son of Shaphan and to Gemariah son of Hilkiah, whom Zedekiah king of Judah sent to King Nebuchadnezzar in Babylon" (Jer. 29:3). Once again, God used the faithfulness of a father's commitment to the Word of God to build a legacy into his own sons. His second son, Elasah, was entrusted with words from the Lord through the prophet Jeremiah to take to King Nebuchadnezzar. There could be no greater joy to godly parents than to see their children loving the Lord, living in His Word and being obedient in His service.

Gemariah, son of Shaphan

The impact of the life of this Hidden Hero did not stop there. Look now at his grandson, the third generation. This young man heard the prophecy of the Lord given to Jeremiah; the words touched his heart, and he went directly to the officials of his nation and said, "You must hear the Word of God." Read the extensive record of this legacy, as found in Jer. 36:10–13: "From the room of Gemariah son of Shaphan the secretary, which was in the upper courtyard at the entrance of the New Gate of the temple, Baruch read to all the people at the LORD's temple the words of Jeremiah from the scroll. When Micaiah son of Gemariah, the son of Shaphan, heard all the words of the Lord from the scroll, he went down to the secretary's room in the royal palace, where all the officials were sitting...Micaiah told them everything he had heard Baruch read to the people from the scroll."

Gedaliah, grandson of Shaphan

Don't stop now. Look at another grandson of Shaphan, Gedaliah, who was a ruler over part of the nation that was in exile. "When the commander of the guard found Jeremiah, he said to him, 'The LORD your God decreed this disaster for this place. And now the LORD has brought it about; he has done just as he said he would. All this happened because you people sinned against the LORD and did not obey him. But today I am freeing you from the chains on your wrists. Come with me to Babylon, if you like, and I will look after you; but if you do not want to, then don't come. Look, the whole country lies before you; go wherever you please.' However, before Jeremiah turned to go, Nebuzaradan added, '*Go back to Gedaliah son of Ahikam, the son of Shaphan* [italics mine], whom the king of Babylon has appointed over the towns of Judah, and live with him among the people, or go anywhere else you please.' Then the commander gave him provisions and a present and let him go" (Jer. 40:2–5).

Jaazaniah, son of Shaphan

Finally, I want to show you a principle that every godly family needs to understand. Proverbs 22:6 says, "Train a child in the way he should go, and when he is old he will not turn from it." This is a biblical principle, not a promise. The principle was realized in most of Shaphan's children, but at least one strayed from his father's example. In the book of Ezekiel, God revealed to His prophet that leaders were worshipping animal deities. One son of Shaphan, Jaazaniah, ignored the teaching of his parents and chose to reject God's Word, living instead in his self-made religion. Here is the truth that must be understood: Jaazaniah's departure from the Word of God was because of his choice, not because Shaphan left his son's spiritual life to chance.

When parents lead by example, the principle of God indicates that our children will not depart from the divine design you provide for them. You become their Hidden Hero, and if by choice, not by chance, you have a child depart from this path, you should not live under condemnation or guilt but live under the mighty grace of God, asking the Lord to do whatever necessary to bring His truth to his life and ask Him to give him a heart to receive the truth.

Finally, we recognize in the life of our Hidden Hero that the priority of the Word of God was not just for himself, his king, or even his family. Shaphan, carrying God's sacred message from the temple to the throne room and placing it before the king, reconnected the people with the voice of their Lord. Even today, the Bible connects people with God no matter what language, no matter where they are, no matter their social status, no matter what their backgrounds may be. In almost every hotel room, in every bookstore, in nearly every home in much of the world, in the most unlikely places, the Word of God is present. Shaphan connected the king to the Word of God, but the Word of God connects the world to the Author of our faith. In the process, the Word connects us to others in a global community of believers.

Not long ago, our church sent two mission teams to Europe. One led a worship workshop in Gyor, Hungary. The other participated in an evangelistic English camp in Moscow, Russia. When the teams returned home, members of the Hungarian team said to the Russian team, "We've got this song you have to hear." Members of the Russian team said almost the same thing, "We heard this song in Moscow, and we think you're going to like it." When the Hungarian team played the song, members of the Russian team were stunned. They said, "That's *our* song!" It was the same song they had become so excited about in Moscow. The song, which spoke of the ancient promise of God's love, was rushing across the continent. New believers in Russia and church members in Hungary had come to our teams and asked each of them to translate the Russian and Hungarian into English so we'd be able to sing the song together. This "new" song is indeed *our* song. And it's Shaphan's song, for it speaks of the enduring words—once lost in a trampled temple, now found to illuminate the hearts and minds of all who seek the Word and work of our God:

Ancient Words

Holy words long preserved
for our walk in this world,
They resound with God's own heart
Oh, let the ancient words impart.

Words of life, words of hope
Give us strength, help us cope
In this world, where e'er we roam
Ancient words will guide us home.

CHORUS:
Ancient words ever true
Changing me, and changing you.
We have come with open hearts
Oh let the ancient words impart.

Holy words of our faith
Handed down to this age
Came to us through sacrifice
Oh heed the faithful words of Christ.

Holy words long preserved
For our walk in this world.
They resound with God's own heart
Oh let the ancient words impart.[1]

(Lynn DeShazo, 2001, Integrity's Hosanna Music)

A Modern-Day Hidden Hero

My introduction to Tommy was seeing him pull up to church with a vanload of teenagers who had been hanging out on the street. I would later find out that Tommy and his wife, Cindy, would go by the local youth hostel each week to provide transportation to any student who wanted to join them for church. For years, this Hidden Hero consistently and quietly made it his ministry to offer a ride to young people that most of the world would shun. They dressed differently from most of the rest of the church. They had different-colored hair (and I mean many different colors on each different head). They were pierced in places that would make it difficult for normal people to function. Not to mention the language of Tommy's congregation...this brought a new dimension to the question, "Is that Greek or Hebrew?" The amazing truth of this weekly ministry was that scores of these kids gave their lives to Christ as a result of Tommy's witness.

After months of watching this faithful man and his wife bring to church these runaway street kids who had found their way to the beaches of Fort Lauderdale, I asked Tommy to share with me about how he got involved in this ministry. He told me his own story of a difficult life, set in a drug culture and compounded by a rebellious heart. He told me how God used the Bible to change his heart and change his life. Over the years, I have watched Tommy and have seen one of the most consistent Christian men in our church. What was the secret of this modern-day Hidden Hero? The answer is simple:

Tommy not only developed the discipline of reading the Word of God daily, but he also sought to live in active obedience to the truth he was taught. The result was that God found an ordinary man with a submitted heart, who at the right time and through the power of Christ was able to accomplish an extraordinary ministry. Thank you, Tommy, for being a modern-day Shaphan, a man who loves the Word of God.

CHAPTER 2

Jubal: An Instrument of Praise

In April 2005, a 305-year-old violin was sold at the famed Christie's auction house in New York for $2.2 million. Setting a "world auction record for a musical instrument," the Stradivarius violin, dating to 1699, drew double the estimated bid. The Christie's specialist for musical instruments provided this understated assessment: "Like a Botticelli or a Rembrandt portrait the instruments of Antonio Stradivari were coveted works of art from the moment of their creation."[2] The previous record-holder? Also a Stradivarius violin.

The reason for the remarkable price is that the cherished instruments are closely held by those who have them and rarely are given up for sale. For the one who can afford the instrument (or the virtuoso artist who cannot afford *not* to have one), a Stradivarius is priceless. During the extended years of his artistry at his Italian workshop in Cremona (1665–1736), Stradivari crafted more than 1,100 stringed instruments, more than half of which are known to still be in existence today.[3] While these instruments share certain Stradivari distinctives, each one has become legendary in its own right, with specific violins acquiring "names, histories, and almost supernatural reputations."[4] The reputations, apparently, are well-deserved. "Why are Stradivarius instruments so highly prized? The most important reason by far is their sound. The best Strads have a rich, refined, resonant sound from the lowest notes to the highest. They're versatile: the same instrument can produce a dark, deep, velvety sound, or a stunningly brilliant sound. And they're powerful. A striking characteristic of Strads is that their sound seems to blossom, so that even over great distances they project clearly and beautifully."[5] No other violin maker has been able to duplicate the uniqueness of these instruments.

One musicologist who has dedicated himself to duplicating the Stradivarius for a quarter of a century notes, "A Stradivari sound is lively. It flickers, it constantly trembles, it moves like candlelight."[6] For three centuries, experts have conjectured about what makes this particular violin such an outstanding instrument, one that actually makes the artist better than he really is. Specialists still search for the secret of Stradivari. Even Sherlock Holmes, the fictional detective who sleuthed out a few Hidden Heroes of his own, is said to have owned a Stradivarius violin in the quest of its mystery. Some have suggested that the quality of a Stradivarius can be attributed to the humidity in the town of Cremona where the violins were made. Others say the wood contains a special sugar from fruit trees. Some credited the chemical qualities pressed into the wood during the time when it was part of a frozen forest. One of the most recent, and most intriguing, theories of the secret is that Antonio Stradivari solemnly carved the wood for his violins from an aging cathedral where the praises of God once resounded.

The exact secret may never be known. Stradivari's secret is somewhat like the secret of this chapter's Hidden Hero, a man named Jubal. Never heard of him? That could be because he's only mentioned once in the Bible. So many other events were sweeping by in the first few chapters of Genesis—creation of the solar system and the world, creation of people, the first family feud—that it can be easy to miss this quiet character.

Strings of the Harp

Jubal is a Hidden Hero not because of what he personally did for the Lord but because of how the Lord used what he did for all mankind. According to Genesis 4:21, he was "the father of all who play the harp and flute." He was the inventor of instrumental music, and his name is associated with the first time any kind of music is mentioned in the biblical record.

There were a lot of firsts in those first chapters of the first book of the Bible. Jubal's father was Lamech, who was the first to marry two wives. Though he sinned by marrying two wives, he was blessed with children by both. The sons of Lamech lived to be famous in their generation, not necessarily for their piety but for their ingenuity. They were not only men of business but also men skilled with the ability to invent and create.

Jabal, the firstborn, was a famous shepherd. He delighted in keeping cattle, and was so happy in devising methods of doing it most effectively and instructing others in those inventive methods. He is referred as the first shepherd, a role so important that one day Jesus would be called the "great Shepherd" (Heb. 13:20). Jubal, the middle brother, was famous for his invention of instrumental music. He invented the very first musical instruments, including both stringed instruments and woodwinds. He is considered the first to introduce the cultured arts into our society. Several instruments—including harps, lyres, and a pair of silver flutes—were discovered in a royal cemetery near the ancient Middle Eastern settlement of Ur,[7] the likely home of Adam's tribe, not far from Eden. The two men had a half-brother, Tubal, who was known for his ironwork and bronze tools. Each of the three names Lamech gave to sons has the same root word: "to lead," "to bring forth," or "to be fruitful."

Some commentators speak of Lamech and his sons only in negative terms, because they were from the line of Cain.

Lamech's character was certainly questionable, but biblical history is replete with sons who chose not to follow the unfortunate ways of their fathers. These scholars seem to draw some strong conclusions from just one verse in the Bible, which itself is not very conclusive—except to conclude that Jubal had a softer spirit, one more comfortable with music and poetry than with sticks and stones.

Although we do not hear about Jubal ever again after verse 21, his legacy is etched throughout the Word of God. Only five verses later in Genesis, the historian of the Hebrews tells us: "At that time men began to call on the name of the LORD" (Genesis 4:26). Where his father Lamech had sought to rule with a sword, Jubal knew that the way of the heart was found in a song.

In our church, we have an orchestra that meets two hours before the service to prepare their instruments, carrying forward this great tradition of instrumental song. Some of the players are high school students, continuing to practice a craft they might have learned as part of a school band. Some of my favorite players are those who are much older, having been away from the instruments of their youth for decades. One day, they decided to dust off that old French horn or restring that guitar in the closet and join the orchestra. Another one of my great delights is to see our teenagers coming to church carrying their guitars and modeling worship in their private moments of devotion and in praise among their peers, playing not to please an audience but out of adoration for the Lord.

All these players follow the pattern of David, who used the music of a harp to soothe King Saul's anger. David himself set aside the sons of Asaph for ministry with harps, lyres, and cymbals (1 Chron. 25:1). King David also gave instruction to us in the book of Psalms, telling us over and over again to give thanks to God with stringed instruments, percussion, woodwinds, and brass. David, like Jubal, was well-acquainted with the mechanics of music and the construction of instruments.

When his son Solomon became king, the celebrants praised God with four thousand musical instruments that "David himself had made for the purpose of praising God." By the time David crowned his son, he was quite old; those instruments must have been something special to have endured such a long time in the winds and sands of the Judean desert.[8]

The harp, one of those instruments said to be invented by Jubal, has an enduring presence—from the first few chapters of Genesis to the last few chapters of Revelation. So strong was Jubal's legacy that the *Oxford Companion to Music* notes, "The harp is ancient and universal; there is a record of it, in some form, in every age of human history and in every place inhabited by man or spirits—except Hell."[9] The stringed instruments and woodwinds Jubal invented took on many forms as Jubal's forebears built on his creativity. The Old Testament mentions castanets (the word actually means "chestnuts," which were struck together to create music), cornets, cymbals, drums, timbrels, tambourines, dulcimers, trumpets, and more. The well-named "psaltery," the unusually named "zither," and the familiar "viol" were much like the lyre and harp.

Strings of the Heart

Notice that the passage from Chronicles not only speaks of the instruments David made but also why he made them: for the purpose of praising God. We don't know what motivated Jubal to hollow out his first flute or set string to wood on his first harp. A musical instrument is completely objective. The instrument stands without intent of its own; it takes a player to select the song that will be played. Some play their music to make a political statement. Some play to woo the opposite sex. Some play for a paycheck (Cole Porter famously said, "My sole inspiration is a telephone call from a producer.") But many play as an expression of praise to their God. George Frederic Handel, who wrote *The Messiah* in just three weeks, proclaimed through tears upon its completion, "I do believe I have seen all of Heaven before me, and the great God Himself."

As he read through the Chronicles in a Bible commentary published by Martin Luther, Bach wrote in his own hand a note in the margin that David's establishment of worship through instruments is "the true foundation of all God-pleasing church music."[10] Each of Bach's surviving manuscripts begins with the letters J.J. and ends with S.D.G.: *Jesu Juva* (Latin for "Jesus, help me!") and *Soli de Gloria* (Latin for "To God alone the glory"). Bach, though a perfectionist ever humble in his art, gave praise to God and humor to himself. When asked about the difficulty of playing the organ, he demurred, saying, "Playing the organ is easy; all you have to do is put your fingers on the right keys at the right times."[11]

My orchestra director, Stephen, says such an understanding of the power and privilege of instrumental music was not always prevalent in Christendom. Although the chosen ones of God clearly played instruments in their worship from the time described in the fourth chapter of Genesis, at some point instruments fell out of favor. Scholar David W. Music (his real name!) says, "The Christian church has a long history of alternately embracing and rejecting musical instruments for worship." Instruments were uncommon, even in the earliest churches, perhaps due to the poverty of the worshippers or the loud sounds that may have given away their secret meeting locations in times of imperial persecution.

Music notes, "If the New Testament was ambivalent about the use of instruments by the church, the Church Fathers were not....they were practically unanimous in their rejecting musical instruments."[12] John Calvin said, "Musical instruments in celebrating the praises of God would be no more suitable than the burning of incense, the lighting of lamps, and the restoration of the other shadows of the law."[13] Beethoven himself is said to have preferred a cappella music in the cathedral, with instrumental music appropriate only for the theater. Even John Wesley, the great hymn writer, said, "I have no objection to instruments of music in our chapels, provided they are neither heard nor seen."[14] Some might think these men were speaking with regard to the Roman church, but Catholic parishes were required to have special papal permission before they were allowed to use any kind of instrument in worship.

Even Charles Spurgeon, the great evangelist and commentator on the Psalms, said instruments were "childish" expressions of faith, saying resolutely, "We do not need them. They would hinder rather than help our praise." (One reporter noted that in his twenty years as pulpiteer at the Metropolitan Baptist Church—speaking to twenty thousand people each Sunday—Spurgeon never allowed instrumental music in his services.) The reasons for rejecting instrumental music were as myriad as the instruments themselves. Some people objected to worldly associations with music, from the Roman temples of the first century to the theatrical orchestrations of the sixteenth century to the late-night jazz clubs of the twentieth century.

Thankfully, God has brought back to us the power of instrumental music in our time. Augustine likened the chords of instrumental music to the harmony of God's people, with many voices blending into one symphonic expression of praise and purpose. Martin Luther, a reformer in so many other ways, pronounced that if it meant reaching young people, he would use whatever sounds possible, including instruments. Choir conductors began to use instruments for pragmatic reasons, either to duplicate the full range of vocals for smaller choirs or in bigger rooms or to provide a reliable pitch and key standard for difficult compositions. Soon, these conductors and other church leaders realized that the instrumental music itself could be an act of worship. This wasn't such a difficult discovery; all they needed to do was to look at the first book of the Bible.

This doesn't assume that the motives for music are always well-placed. Without question, what God has made for creative good is often counterfeited by forces that seek to falsify His greatest gifts. It's possible for us to give a bad name to the best of God's creation. This reminds me of the joke Bob Hope once told, while describing comedienne Phyllis Diller playing the piano: "When she started to play, Steinway himself personally came down and rubbed his name off the piano." When we don't properly handle the gifts God has given us, it's possible that His signature is erased from the work we produce. Sometimes, we get in the way of the song God desires to play through our lives. Speaking to one of his trumpet players, conductor Arturo Toscanini yelled, "God tells me how the music should sound, but you stand in the way!" Do we stand in the way of God's perfect compositions? Or do we play our best, praying for His best, allowing His presence and power to combine for a symphony of His mercy and grace. Too often, we try to forge forward with our own charts, forgetting the One who has made the music possible and forgetting why the instruments were made.

Another Stradivari instrument was in the news recently. A young nurse, on her way to see a patient, noticed a piece of wood propped up against a Dumpster. Her boyfriend was a cabinetmaker, so Melanie Stevens was always on the lookout for discarded but usable wood. When she approached the Dumpster, she noticed that the discarded wood was a stringed instrument of some type. She loaded it up, took it home, and asked her boyfriend to turn it into a compact disc rack or something useful like that. Only a few days later, while reading the newspaper, did Stevens realize that the instrument she had discovered was a 320-year-old 1664 cello, one of only sixty built by Antonio Stradivari. Even rarer than a Stradivari violin, the prized cello of the Los Angeles Philharmonic almost became a CD holder! The cello had been left on a front porch by the philharmonic's principal cellist. Security cameras from a nearby home showed someone stopping at the porch, loading the cello on a bicycle, and stealing it away. The thief must have decided the battered instrument was worthless, not even bothering to pawn it. The cello was repaired and returned to its rightful place at the Walt Disney Concert Hall.

As amazing as this true story is, it's apparently not an isolated case. Artists frequently lose their instruments: YoYo Ma forgot his multimillion dollar Stradivari cello in a New York City taxi in 2002. Just months before Melanie Stevens' Dumpster discovery, violinist Gidon Kremer left his Guarneri del Gesu (also worth millions of dollars) on a train.[15] Yes, a lost instrument is disconcerting, but even more devastating is an instrument that has lost its purpose. The real tragedy of a lost instrument is when the music is played but the Master Musician is forgotten.

Marian Evans, the writer who took the pen name George Eliot, expressed this when she wrote "The Legend of Jubal" in 1869.[16] (Even though the Bible only gives Jubal one line, George Eliot offered more than eight hundred lines of poetry to extol his faith and fate!) Eliot's story is just poetic conjecture; we don't really know what happened to Jubal beyond Genesis 4:21. But the tale becomes interesting, as through her imagination she describes the first discovery of musical instruments. As Jubal listened to his older brother's building endeavors, he heard something wonderfully rhythmic. With each strike of the hammer, Jubal heard a song:

> Each gave new tones, the revelations dim
> Of some external soul that spoke for him:
> The hollow vessel's clang, the clash, the boom,
> Like light that makes wide spiritual room
> And skyey spaces in the spaceless thought,
> To Jubal such enlarged passion brought,
> That love, hope, rage, and all experience,
> Were fused in vaster being, fetching thence
> Concords and discords, cadences and cries

That seemed from some world-shrouded soul
   to rise,
Some rapture more intense, some mightier rage,
Some living sea that burst the bounds of man's
   brief age.

Jubal borrows a few of his brother's tools, carves a bow for his harp, hollows out a branch for his flute, and quietly begins to practice his instruments.

Alone amid the hills at first he tried
His winged song; then with adoring pride
And bridegroom's joy at leading forth his bride,
He said, "This wonder which my soul hath found,
This heart of music in the might of sound,
Shall forthwith be the share of all our race,
And like the morning gladden common space:
The song shall spread and swell as rivers do,
And I will teach our youth with skill to woo
This living lyre, to know its secret will;
Its fine division of the good and ill.
So shall men call me sire of harmony,
And where great Song is, there my life shall be.

In Eliot's version of the story, Jubal, having established the gift of music among his own people, travels to faraway lands to teach others the majesty of music. When he returns generations later, he finds his people immersed in song, even though they don't always know why. Even from far away, he hears the melody and watches his artistic heirs who have become so proficient on the instruments he had created. He can't wait to be among them again, telling stories of all he had seen in his travels, reminding them of his inspiration from God and playing alongside these accomplished musicians in his own homeland. Proclaiming his identity, he says, "I am Jubal, the one who made the harp and the flute." But no one believes him. For them, Jubal is a myth, a legend, someone about whom fathers and uncles tell fireside stories. For anyone to claim to be Jubal is a mockery. Yet he says, "I am Jubal, I! I made the lyre!" At that, his countrymen—sons of the sons of his brothers—pounce upon him and pummel him to lifelessness with their flutes, flutes Jubal himself had made. The irony resounds to this day; we often take God's creative gift and fashion it into something He never intended.

An instrument without a heart is just a piece of metal or wood. Several years ago, my friend Don Moen came to our church and recorded an evening of praise for Integrity Music. Don is an accomplished pianist, songwriter, and worship leader. Millions have voiced their faith in God with words he wrote as they sing his songs, like "Give Thanks," "Blessed Be the Name of the Lord," or "God Will Make a Way." But one thing I love about Don is that he understands the depth of power in instrumental music to sway the spirits of men to the hope of God. One of the songs on the album we recorded that night was called "Be Still My Soul," written by another friend of mine, Kim Noblitt, who was serving as our worship leader at the time. Don decided the best way to communicate the ideal of "being still at soul" was through the woodwind worship of Justo Almario. The words of Kim's song were powerful, but they were made personal and profound by the presence of God as Justo played his flute with the spirit and skill God had given him.

Strings of Hope

The flute is among the many instruments that appear in the Psalms. These instruments appear most strongly and poignantly in the last psalm, number 150. The term "psalm," from the Greek *psalmos*, actually entails the sense of a song integrally accompanied by an instrument. The literal meaning of the root word, the verb *psallo*, is to strike or pluck a string as on a harp.

Psalm 150 begins with a purpose statement: "Praise the Lord!" In the original language, this was literally "Hallel u Yah," and many of us today speak Hebrew without even knowing it when we exclaim our praise to the Lord with hallelujahs. This "hallel u yah" has even more force, directing a strong command to the reader (or listeners): "*You* praise the Lord." That's what the "u" in the middle is, and why we often hear this phrase translated as "praise *ye* the Lord." The author of the ultimate psalm then specifies *where* we are to express praise: "Praise God in his sanctuary; praise him in his mighty heavens" (verse 1). Then he says *why* we are to express praise, "for his acts of power, praise him for his surpassing greatness" (verse 2). Then the psalmist tells us *how* to praise God in verses 3–5:

> Praise him with the sounding of the trumpet,
>   praise him with the harp and lyre,
>   praise him with tambourine and dancing,
>   praise him with the strings and flute,
>   praise him with the clash of cymbals,
>   praise him with resounding cymbals.

In the final verse, the psalmist reveals *who* is to express such adoration: "Let everything that has breath praise the LORD. Praise the LORD!" It's not often that I quote King James English, but the power of this psalm is so profound: "Praise ye the Lord...let everything that hath breath praise ye the Lord!" (KJV). That proclamation of praise translates across time, though, and it's just as profound in a modern paraphrase. I like how *The Message* expresses this same psalm:

> Hallelujah! Praise God in His holy house of worship,
>   praise Him under the open skies;
> Praise Him for his acts of power, praise Him for
>   his magnificent greatness;

> Praise with a blast on the trumpet, praise by strumming soft strings;
> Praise Him with castanets and dance, praise Him with banjo and flute;
> Praise Him with cymbals and a big bass drum, praise Him with fiddles and mandolin.
> Let every living, breathing creature praise God! Hallelujah![17]

This most modern of versions begins and ends the psalm with the most ancient of praises: "Hallel u Yah." But then the author who paraphrased the psalm, Eugene Peterson, speaks of the variety of voices with which we express our praise: from the tender "strumming soft strings" to the bold "big bass drum." A trumpet blast, castanets and dancing, mandolins and banjos. One of our accompanists, Dr. Nina Wood-Charles, who has a doctorate in ethnomusicology, tells me this psalm could be intended to represent the promised return of every people to the praises of God. Who wouldn't want to be part of that celebration? This seems to be a global event: Latino castanets, banjos from Africa (known there as banzas, banjars, banias, or bangoes),[18] mandolins and fiddles from Middle Europe, drums from Asia. And, of course, harps and flutes from the beginning of time.

One early church father described the scene as this, that all people and all creation, "after the disunion and disorder caused by sin have been removed, are harmoniously united for one choral dance, and the chorus of mankind concerting with the angel chorus are become one cymbal of divine praise, and the final song of victory shall salute God, the triumphant Conqueror, with shouts of joy."[19]

Think of the great music that moves your heart. Beethoven. Mozart. A patriotic anthem. A pop music love song. The greatest of them all cannot compare to a psalm such as this one, praising the Greatest of Them All. This expression would be so much less without the power and diversity of the instruments and voices described in the psalm. For a contemporary parallel, one commentator suggests that "The Hallelujah Chorus," Handel's masterpiece from *The Messiah*, "would never stir us as it does without the many human voices sounding together in majesty and without the harmony of all the musical instruments that we can employ today. These sing forth on the strings of the violin, and resonate deeply on the heart-shattering bass of the great array of drums, enhancing the words of exultant praise. So, too, in this final psalm every voice in heaven and earth, and every musical instrument that human ingenuity has produced are called upon to join in the praise of the Living God."[20]

This closely aligns with the portrayal of Jubal's instrument, the harp, in the book of Revelation. In three different places in this climactic book of the Bible, the victorious faithful use the harp to express unending praise to God. In chapter 5, the elders dramatically hold harps and "the prayers of God's people" (verse 8) as they sing to the Lamb, "You are worthy to take the scroll and break its seals and open it. For you were killed, and your blood has ransomed people for God from every tribe and language and people and nation. And you have caused them to become God's Kingdom and his priests. And they will reign on the earth" (Rev. 5:9–10 NLT). In Rev. 15:3–4 (also NLT), the text specifies that the harps had been given to them by God Himself so they could sing,

> Great and marvelous are your actions,
> Lord God Almighty. Just and true are your ways,
> O King of the nations.
> Who will not fear, O Lord, and glorify your name?
> For you alone are holy. All nations will come and worship
>   before you,
> for your righteous deeds have been revealed.

When days are dark and difficult, these words are words of powerful hope. Just as one who listens to music may be swayed by the sound of the notes and rhythms, the one who listens to this eternal symphony of praise is moved by the dramatic crescendo of God's presence among men.

Jubal was an inventor, the first to give us musical instruments. God used Jubal's invention to bring honor and glory to His name. The apostle Paul challenges us to have our instruments of witness ready. It's not enough just to have the instrument; we must be prepared to voice the Song of the Redeemed. Here's what Paul says: "If musical instruments—flutes, say, or harps –aren't played so that each note is distinct and in tune, how will anyone be able to catch the melody and enjoy the music? If the trumpet call can't be distinguished, will anyone show up for the battle? So if you speak in a way no one can understand, what's the point of opening your mouth?" (1 Cor. 14:7–9 Message). What do you have in your life that God wants to use to bring honor and glory to His name? Don't keep it hidden any longer.

A Modern-Day Hidden Hero

Try to think for a moment what music would be like without an instrument. Don't get me wrong; I love a good a cappella number as much as the next guy, but seriously…if that is all we had, what would our world be like today? About the only good thing I can think that would come from a world without instruments is perhaps I could drive my car without the bass of some guy's radio three blocks away shattering my windshield! Every time I think of Jubal, the Hidden Hero of this chapter, my mind takes me back to the first time I saw an eight-year-old boy standing before about three thousand people and playing his violin in a way that would make most professionals envious. Julian has always been gifted, not just in his music but also in the power of God's Spirit that rests upon his life.

As a prodigy, this young man had an intensity about him that I have never witnessed in other children. He took his music seriously, but he also took his relationship to Christ seriously. As Julian grew to be a young man, his music and maturity in Christ also developed at an explosive pace. Each time Julian would stand before the congregation, the people would be mesmerized by both his skill and his composure. By the time Julian was eighteen, he was concertmaster for the internationally acclaimed Fort Lauderdale Christmas Pageant. You would think I would tell you that Julian is playing today at Carnegie Hall, but that is not the case. I remember the day Julian came to me and shared his plans for the future. "I'm going to enlist in the Marines. They will allow me to go to college and come out of my education as an officer." I tried to not allow my shocked expression to reveal the amazement I sensed in hearing this decision. "What about your music?" I asked him. "God gave me the ability to play, and I will always play for Him. But I believe there is more that He wants to do in my life. To serve my country while also serving my Savior would be a great honor."

I asked Julian that day what the greatest desire of his heart would be as he made this decision. Without a pause, this young Hidden Hero said, "To see my dad come to faith in Christ." Today, I am forever thankful for Jubal and his invention of instrumental music, because this one gift to our society allowed a young Hidden Hero in Fort Lauderdale to provide a melodious witness for the Savior he loves.

CHAPTER 3

Jehosheba: The Messianic Bloodline

✦

This story sounds like something out of a novel: "When Athaliah the mother of Ahaziah saw that her son was dead, she proceeded to destroy the whole royal family. But Jehosheba, the daughter of King Jehoram and sister of Ahaziah, took Joash son of Ahaziah and stole him away from among the royal princes, who were about to be murdered. She put him and his nurse in a bedroom to hide him from Athaliah; so he was not killed. He remained hidden with his nurse at the temple of the LORD for six years while Athaliah ruled the land" (2 Kings 11:1–3).

A brave woman from Holland, joined by members of her family, risked their lives to hide Jewish people from a satanically driven madman in World War II. The story of Corrie ten Boom is well documented; she is remembered in history as one of the bravest women the world has ever known, risking her own life and suffering in prison for the sole purpose of rescuing others from Hitler and his attempted genocide of the Jewish race. Ten Boom often referred to the fact that she knew God was using her to accomplish His purpose at that time in history. During the time she was rescuing Jewish families she never took time to worry. "Worry does not empty tomorrow of its sorrow; it empties today of its strength," ten Boom said.

However, long before God had prepared Corrie ten Boom to take action to preserve precious lives, He prepared a little known woman in the Bible to perform one of the most heroic acts and significant rescues in the entire Bible. To Jehosheba, the world must have looked out of control in 841 B.C. This young woman was a princess in the Davidic lineage, the wife of the high priest. As she watched with horror during a reign of terror, one by one the men in the bloodline of King David were murdered. Jehu was dispatched by God to issue judgment on the house of sinful and wicked Ahab and his descendants. He then killed what many believe to be the wickedest woman of the Bible, Jezebel. The judgment did not stop there, as Jehu went throughout the land destroying all in the house of Ahab, who ruled the more evil nation of the divided kingdom. Scripture tells us in 2 Chronicles 22:9: "So there was no one in the house of Ahaziah powerful enough to retain the kingdom" of Judah.

Enter wicked Queen Athaliah. When this woman heard that most of the royal heirs had been destroyed, she seized what she considered to be her greatest opportunity. This woman ordered her own grandchildren murdered so she could have the throne all to herself and never have to worry about a rival. She assumed the throne and began to reign over the people of God. However, she made one tragic mistake in her quest for power. She failed to recognize the fact that God had prepared Jehosheba, His Hidden Hero, for this moment in history.

Evil Intentions

King Ahaziah, only in his early twenties, had inherited the throne as the only surviving son of Jehoram. Jehoram himself had a history of evil, completely unlike the father from whom he inherited the throne, the good king Jehoshaphat. As soon as

Jehoshaphat died, Jerhoram assumed the throne and had his brothers killed. He married a daughter of Israel's evil king Ahab, Athaliah, and his extreme wickedness caused significant tension in God's covenant between Judah and the house of David. The Bible says that Jehoram finally died to "no one's regret." (2 Chron. 21:20). So hated by his own people was Jehoram that he was buried not with the kings who had preceded him but in a place of great disgrace.

By the time Jehoram was dead, his youngest son, Ahaziah, was the only choice for king since Jehoram had killed all his own brothers, and all of his own sons (besides Ahaziah) had already been killed in battle. Ahaziah ruled only one year, practicing the same deceit and wickedness as his father, following the ways of evil Ahab.

Ahaziah was dispatched by Jehoshaphat's son, Jehu, who was anointed as king of Israel by the prophet Elisha. Upon Ahaziah's death, his mother took her treacherous opportunity. This evil-hearted daughter of one of the wickedest kings in all of Israel, Ahab, saw her chance as she immediately promoted herself to the throne and insured that she would face no opposition. Obviously, Satan used one of his greatest weapons in securing the help of Queen Athaliah, the sin of a prideful heart. On the surface she appears to be just one madwoman whose obsession with power drives her terrorist actions. That is exactly what Satan wants you to think. He wants us to always dismiss the fact that he is the "prince of the power of the air" and constantly placing the temptation before mankind. James reminds us that once we conceive sin into our heart, death is born in our lives. The intention of Satan has always been to destroy the witness of God, to usurp His power, His authority, even His throne.

This story is a classic example of the work of the enemy in our own lives today. If Satan can destroy the witness and life of Christ that resides in you, then he can effectively move one step closer to his goal of wresting the power from God and ultimately becoming the "Unholy One of the Universe." Yes, on the surface it appears to only be one woman's bloodthirsty quest for power, but upon closer examination we begin to see the reality and expose the true intentions of Satan. The true intention of Satan in his use of Athaliah as his pawn was to absolutely destroy and break the royal line of the Messiah.

Remember, God had already promised in His Word: "Your house and your kingdom will endure forever before me; your throne will be established forever" (2 Sam. 7:16). Through Isaiah, the covenant was assured:

> Of the increase of his government and peace
> there will be no end.
> He will reign on David's throne
> and over his kingdom,
> establishing and upholding it
> with justice and righteousness
> from that time on and forever.
> The zeal of the LORD Almighty
> will accomplish this. (Isa. 9:7)

Now, at least on the surface, it appears that Satan has succeeded and destroyed the lineage of David. With the destruction of this bloodline, we would also have the destruction of the promise of the Messiah. This is now the picture of the great struggle that takes place every day in every corner of the world in every heart of every person who desires to place Jesus as the true King of Kings and Lord of Lords. This is the classic struggle between good and evil, between Satan and God. It is the struggle each of us should understand and prepare to overcome, in His power.

We have two women who represent the same principles of good and evil: Athaliah, the pawn in the hand of Satan, and Jehosheba, a humble servant available for God's purposes...a true Hidden Hero. The scene is set. Satan has a staggering plan indeed. The consequences could be unimaginable. If Satan's plan is successful, the bloodline of David would be destroyed and God's promised Messiah could never be born. What is Satan attempting to do in your life that on the surface seems insignificant? If you were to see the full context of his scheme, how is it that he's trying to destroy you and all that you love? The stakes are high indeed, for the people of God in the time of Jehosheba and for the people of God today.

God's Intervention

If that's your struggle today, you should know that God has a purpose and a plan. Even in the midst of adversity brought on by the enemy, God is working on your behalf. Remember His promise through Isaiah:

> I make known the end from the beginning,
>   from ancient times, what is still to come.
> I say: My purpose will stand,
>   and I will do all that I please.
> From the east I summon a bird of prey;
>   from a far-off land, a man to fulfill my purpose.
> What I have said, that will I bring about;
>   what I have planned, that will I do. (Isa. 46:10–11)

What we must understand in this classic struggle of good and evil is this one principle: Nothing will stop the purpose of God from being accomplished. You cannot outrun Him, you cannot outsmart Him, you cannot outmaneuver Him, and you cannot outshine Him. The key truths of this story are that even though the world may appear to be out of control, God is in control, and His purpose will prevail.

At the same time Satan was preparing the wicked heart of Athaliah to serve his evil intentions, God was preparing the tender, humble heart of a woman who was surrendered to His perfect will. Her name was Jehosheba. She was not only the stepdaughter of the wicked queen, but she was also the wife of the high priest, Jehoiada. This was a woman who by faith was able to overcome her fears. Think about this for a moment. Her stepmother had already killed nearly all her own grandchildren in order to secure her place on the throne. Do you think for a moment she would have hesitated to destroy Jehosheba? Our faith does not mean that we will not have fear. It simply means we will not be paralyzed by the fear, and we will be overcomers.

God does nothing by accident but always according to His purpose. Our Hidden Hero grew up in the palace. As a young girl, she no doubt played the game of hide-and-seek with the other children of the court. She knew all the rooms, all the hideouts, and every little corner in which to hide. Now all that knowledge will play a very essential part in rescuing the last remaining seed in the Davidic bloodline. When she saw the crisis, she responded to the need in the power and name of the Lord. After all, that is the nature of a Hidden Hero.

Jehosheba entered the palace and took the year-old baby, her nephew Joash, away from the rest of the king's sons who were being murdered: "But Jehosheba, the daughter of King Jehoram and sister of Ahaziah, took Joash son of Ahaziah and stole him away from among the royal princes, who were about to be murdered. She put him and his nurse in a bedroom to hide him from Athaliah; so he was not killed" (2 Kings 11:2).

She took the baby and his nurse and hid them in what we would call a storage closet for bed frames and mattresses. We know from historians that this room was never used for dwelling, and so it would be a logical place to temporarily hide the young king. Later she took the baby and the nurse into the temple and put them in seclusion and protection for the next six years. In the temple, our Hidden Hero was used of God to intervene and stop the intended plan of Satan. We must never forget that had Jehosheba not acted by faith, Joash would have been killed with the rest of the bloodline, and the Davidic king-

Jehosheba: The Messianic Bloodline

dom would have come to an end. The Redeemer, whom God had promised to all of mankind, would have never been born.

Jehosheba, like Corrie ten Boom, ignored the personal risk to her life in order to save the lives of others. The life she preserved was the end of the line, the last remaining heir to David's throne. After six years of lovingly and spiritually preparing this young man to be king, Jehosheba and her husband, Jehoiada, put an elaborate plan in place to announce to the people that Joash was the rightful ruler of the land. As all the plans were complete and all the support enlisted, the day finally came when it became obvious to all that Satan's intention had been thwarted by God's miraculous intervention. "Jehoiada and his sons brought out the king's son and put the crown on him; they presented him with a copy of the covenant and proclaimed him king. They anointed him and shouted, 'Long live the king!'" (2 Chron. 23:11).

The wicked queen was killed. The kingdom was secure, and so was the bloodline of the Messiah.

There are times in our lives when we must stand and be counted, even if it means risking our own reputation, our worldly possessions, and even our lives. Like Esther and Jehosheba, we must ask ourselves in the dark days of evil, "Has God prepared my life for a time such as this?" I am thankful that Jehosheba was pro-life in a most proactive way. She knew that the life of this young baby, who had been senselessly sentenced to die, could be used to have a great and significant impact on the world in which he lived. As I contemplated the millions of children who have been slaughtered each year in abortion clinics all over America and around the world, I cannot help but wonder how many of those babies Satan destroyed because he knew they would grow to be great and influential men and women who would honor Jesus Christ and bring His light into this world. I thank God for this woman of faith, Jehosheba, a real Hidden Hero who was used by God to intervene and thwart the plan of the enemy.

A Modern-Day Hidden Hero

As I was contemplating the modern-day equivalent of Jehosheba, this great woman of faith, I was directed in my spirit to consider a woman in my own life who has made great sacrifices for the eternal reward. Like Jehosheba, this woman has demonstrated the conviction, faith, and fortitude that make her a true modern-day Hidden Hero.

Allow me to introduce you to Nettie. She is a woman who was born as our nation was coming out of the Great Depression. She didn't have the luxuries and the benefits we enjoy today, but she had something of far greater value: she had great faith in God and a commitment to honor Him in the call of her life as a Christian. She, like Jehosheba, has invested in children her entire life. From my earliest memory I can still recall her coming home from her second job late on Saturday night and putting together all of her teaching materials so she could teach her third graders biblical truths on Sunday morning. She worked five days a week for a doctor and then took a job at a hospital working from 3 to 11 p.m. on Saturday and Sunday in order to help provide for the needs of her family. In spite of this seven-day workweek, I never heard her complain, and she never wavered in her love for Christ and her commitment to provide children the opportunity to grow in truth.

In our home, going to church was not an option. It was a way of life. I could never repay this woman for the foundation of faith she provided for me. It was on that foundation that I found Christ, and it was on that foundation that I answered His call and committed my life to proclaiming His truth to this world. She continues to live today in the same modest, thousand-square foot home in Oklahoma City where she has lived for almost 60 years. It was in that home that she spiritually instructed her four children, and it was in that home that she, like Jehosheba, made sure the next generation would not only have life but also a spiritual purpose for life. She, like her

Old Testament counterpart, realized how essential a spiritual foundation is to the life of an individual and a nation.

Like Jehosheba, she could see the potential in the life of a young boy and gave her life to ensure that potential had the opportunity to be realized. I used to be so angry when her car would pull up to my Little League baseball practice and she would make me leave early so she could take me to my private speech class. She would save her money and pay for me to have private lessons in order to learn and refine the art of communication. She would tell me, "God has given you a gift, and you must prepare to use it for His glory." I resented the intrusion when I was a child. Today, I admire the wisdom and insight God gave this woman and her willingness to act in order to prepare a young man for a God-sized future. She has never enjoyed the "riches" of this world, and yet she would tell you that she is richly blessed. This modern-day Hidden Hero continues to teach the Word of God every Sunday. She continues to look for the children who need protection and to invest her life in them while giving them hope. She is not recognized as a world-famous leader, but she will forever be my hero and, I am so proud to say, my mother.

CHAPTER 4

Joab: Leadership Essential

The church will only fulfill its mission when its leadership is following a leader. Joab, this chapter's Hidden Hero, became a great leader by learning first to be a great follower. You cannot be a great leader until you have learned to be a great follower. As we examine the life of Joab, we will examine characteristics of Joab's leadership that should be a great encouragement to every believer.

Joab appears in biblical history as one of the most accomplished and powerful warriors that Israel ever produced. As we look at some of the key situations of his life, we will discover some secrets of real leadership. Taken as a whole, this man was one the greatest leaders of David's generals, and much of David's success and glory can be credited to this noblest of all his warriors.

Consider his qualifications:

- Brilliant planner and military strategist
- Fearless fighter and resourceful commander
- Confident leader who did not hesitate to confront the king

- Reconciler, as illustrated with David and Absalom
- Great and loyal follower of God's anointed

He didn't develop this resume overnight. Instead, he took a tried and tested path. Five different elements of that path made Joab who he was. First, he understood a leader's responsibility. Consider the words from 1 Chron. 11:1–6, particularly verse 6, which describes the beginning of Joab's military career:

> All Israel came together to David at Hebron and said, "We are your own flesh and blood. In the past, even while Saul was king, you were the one who led Israel on their military campaigns. And the LORD your God said to you, 'You will shepherd my people Israel, and you will become their ruler.' " When all the elders of Israel had come to King David at Hebron, he made a compact with them at Hebron before the LORD, and they anointed David king over Israel, as the LORD had promised through Samuel. David and all the Israelites marched to Jerusalem (that is, Jebus). The Jebusites who lived there said to David, "You will not get in here." Nevertheless, David captured the fortress of Zion, the City of David. David had said, "Whoever leads the attack on the Jebusites will become commander-in-chief." Joab son of Zeruiah went up first, and so he received the command.

This stimulus for the invasion reflected David's wisdom regarding leadership promotions. This incident in the life of Joab reveals the responsibility leaders take for the difficult assignments in life and the results that accompany their decisive actions. Examining the conquest of Jerusalem we find that men from any tribe in Israel had the same opportunity as did Joab; the difference is that Joab acted in regard to this opportunity and was responsible in achieving the victory.

Leadership promotions are reserved for those individuals who earn the title of leader by accepting the responsibility for the assignments placed before them.

Chris is a member of our ministry staff team, called to minister alongside us after serving as chief financial officer for South Florida's largest hospital district. Chris believes leadership is earned; it is not a gift or title to be granted to those who simply have "connections" or relationships with those who grant the promotion. Joab was promoted by King David because he accepted the responsibility. When we consider men to serve as deacons or servant leaders in our fellowship, the decisions are *never* based on popularity or social status; they are based on determining which leaders have proven their servant heart by accepting responsibility and showing they could be counted on in time of need. David's wisdom is obvious in his test of selecting a leader by insisting that he prove himself first. Joab revealed the first principle of true leadership:

1. A leader accepts responsibility for the task that is before him.

Joab had strong work ethic and was more concerned about his duty than his honors. This is such a contrast to so many in our world today. Give them a position of honor, and they will spend their time looking in the mirror seeing how their crown or insignia or robe of honor looks rather than getting busy with their task. They think the position has been given them simply to honor them rather than for them to use their position to help others.

The "Jerusalems" in our world will not be conquered by those whose interests are primarily found in the accolades rather than in taking the responsibility for the assignments of their office.

The second principle of leadership, which we see in the life of this Hidden Hero, is…

2. A leader recognizes the service of others.

Spiritual leaders should be recognized for two areas in their life: their accomplishments and their attitudes. The victory over Jerusalem involved great determination by Joab, our Hidden Hero. The word "nevertheless" shows the kind of determination David and Joab had to take into this battle. In spite of the insults from the Jebusites and in spite of the strong fortification of Jerusalem, Joab went ahead and attacked the city and conquered it. We noted earlier that Joab chose a difficult task when he chose to conquer Jerusalem. Joab was not looking for easy tasks; he was looking for today's task. His determination did not let the difficult tasks discourage him. He had great determination to accomplish the conquest of Jerusalem, and this determination was certainly an important factor for his personal recognition.

If you want to achieve in any area, you will have to have some sanctified determination. Leaders will never achieve recognition for their accomplishments without a strong determination that refuses to be discouraged by the ridicule of others or by the difficulty of the task. Much failure in people's lives is not because of a lack of opportunity or difficulty of the task. Failure to become a leader is too often the result of a lack of determination, but we try to blame other things for our failure to be recognized as a leader. Blame other things if you will for your failure, but the real problem for your failure to accomplish leadership positions in life is often the lack of determination. And until you recognize that problem in your life, you will not know or understand the recognition that comes to a leader.

Just as important as accomplishment is the attitude with which great challenges are faced. True spiritual leaders always receive their recognition in true humility. There is always a sense of being unworthy of the recognition, because a real spiritual leader always acknowledges that the victory comes from the Lord. In 1 Chron. 11:6, there are two illustrations of humility found in Joab's life:

First, in his attitude toward work. Where did Joab go first? The sewer! He went to defeat the Jebusites by going through the city's sewer system that ran out through the walls. The enemy expected to be confronted face to face, and they knew their fortified city was almost unbeatable if the invading army fought with a normal battle plan. The Bible elaborates on the master plan:

> On that day, David said, "Anyone who conquers the Jebusites will have to use the water shaft to reach those 'lame and blind' who are David's enemies." That is why they say, "The 'blind and lame' will not enter the palace." (2 Sam. 5:8)

You will never be the leader God wants you to be until you have the attitude of a spiritual leader, an attitude that says there is no job that is too small or too dirty for me to accomplish.

Second, in his attitude toward honor. The word "received" is a word that means "to present yourself; to humbly accept." Joab would bow before David after David had already reminded the army that the battle was the Lord's. Joab humbly received the position of leader, captain of the entire military kingdom in Israel. He accepted his leadership role in humility, which should be the case for every true spiritual leader. He clearly demonstrated a third principle of leadership:

3. A leader respects authority.

Meanwhile Joab fought against Rabbah of the Ammonites and captured the royal citadel. Joab then sent messengers to David, saying, "I have fought against Rabbah and taken its water supply. Now muster the rest of the troops and besiege the city and capture it. Otherwise I will take the city, and it will be named after me." (2 Sam. 12:26–28)

This is the story of Joab's conquest and capture of the Ammonite capital, Rabbah. This is a clear picture of being steadfast and persevering against one's enemies. For at least nine months, David's army, under the leadership of Joab, had been attempting to starve the capital city Rabbah into submission. Eventually, the military strategy accomplished its purpose, as Scripture reveals. At about the time the city was to fall, Joab captured the city's water supply and immediately sent messengers to report that fact to King David. Joab's loyalty and respect for authority is evident in this passage. Joab wanted the king to receive credit for the victory; he challenged King David to mobilize reinforcements and to join him in the battle. As a faithful and loyal follower and the chief military officer of the king, Joab wanted David to be honored as the conqueror and to have the city renamed after him. This is an obvious reflection on Joab's character as a leader. He has great respect for authority. A leader can never be *over* until he learns to be *under*!

Also, a true spiritual leader *never* touches the glory or honor that rightfully belongs to the king. Joab called for the king to come quickly so he alone would receive the glory and honor. We are reminded of this principle in the Psalms:

> Not to us, O LORD, not to us
> but to your name be the glory,
> because of your love and faithfulness. (Ps.115:1)

This brings us to our fourth principle:

4. A leader has the courage to rebuke.

> Joab was told, "The king is weeping and mourning for Absalom." And for the whole army the victory that

day was turned into mourning, because on that day the troops heard it said, "The king is grieving for his son." The men stole into the city that day as men steal in who are ashamed when they flee from battle. The king covered his face and cried aloud, "O my son Absalom! O Absalom, my son, my son!"

Then Joab went into the house to the king and said, "Today you have humiliated all your men, who have just saved your life and the lives of your sons and daughters and the lives of your wives and concubines. You love those who hate you and hate those who love you. You have made it clear today that the commanders and their men mean nothing to you. I see that you would be pleased if Absalom were alive today and all of us were dead. Now go out and encourage your men. I swear by the LORD that if you don't go out, not a man will be left with you by nightfall. This will be worse for you than all the calamities that have come upon you from your youth till now."

So the king got up and took his seat in the gateway. When the men were told, "The king is sitting in the gateway," they all came before him. (2 Sam. 19:1–8)

One of the most difficult assignments in leadership is in knowing when to confront and rebuke another in order to preserve the integrity of the individual or organization. Joab's courage in confronting and rebuking the king he loved and served is a classic picture of a great leader. Confrontation is perhaps the most difficult assignment of a true leader.

This is a sad picture of King David as an indulgent, permissive parent who needed to be rebuked. It is a pathetic scene that David creates over the death of his rebellious, wicked son Absalom. Hearing the news of Absalom's death shook David, and he was overwhelmed with emotion.

Turning and walking away from everyone standing around the city gates, he began repeatedly crying out for his dead son, "Oh my son Absalom, my son, my son Absalom!" He even cried out to God that he wished he had died instead of Absalom. No doubt everyone under the king's authority who witnessed the shameful scene was utterly surprised at David's irresponsible behavior.

As the army of King David returned and set up camp outside the city, the news of David's unrestrained emotions began to spread and started to adversely affect his troops. Instead of a celebration over the momentous victory, the joy of the occasion was turned into sadness. Hearing the reports of David's uncontrolled mourning caused the soldiers to creep back into the city as though they were a defeated army and had been shamed. David made no attempt to hide his shameful behavior.

Soon David's mourning was reported to our Hidden Hero, Joab. The anger of Joab became so aroused that he could take no more of David's shameful actions. Rushing to David's quarters, Joab confronted and rebuked David, making three charges against him:

> Insensitivity: He had shamed and humiliated his troops who had just saved his life, his kingdom, and the lives of his family members.

> Insult: He was showing love for those who hated him (Absalom) and hate for those who loved him (his army).

> Ingratitude: He was displaying ingratitude toward those who served him, acting as though his soldiers meant nothing to him, as though he would be pleased if Absalom had defeated and killed all of them.

Boldly, Joab rebuked the king and told David to encourage his troops. He warned David that the troops were on the verge of deserting him and that by nightfall there would not be a single soldier left to support him in reestablishing his government when he returned to Jerusalem. He was about to face the crisis of his life, losing the allegiance of all his supporters.

David accepted the rebuke of Joab. As had happened so often in the past, Joab's decisive action and his willingness to confront and rebuke the king ultimately saved David's kingdom. What I love about Joab is that he was not afraid to confront and rebuke the one he loved and served; yet he still respected him enough to first talk to the king and then rebuke him privately. In his rebuke he offered him counsel for making right the wrong; this action is the heart of a true man or woman of God who is a chosen leader in the Kingdom of God.

And this brings us to our fifth and final leadership principle:

5. A leader has reverence for God.

> So the king said to Joab and the army commanders with him, "Go throughout the tribes of Israel from Dan to Beersheba and enroll the fighting men, so that I may know how many there are." But Joab replied to the king, "May the LORD your God multiply the troops a hundred times over, and may the eyes of my lord the king see it. But why does my lord the king want to do such a thing?" The king's word, however, overruled Joab and the army commanders; so they left the presence of the king to enroll the fighting men of Israel. (2 Sam. 24:2–4)

God allowed Satan to tempt David to take the census. A false pride and trust in the power of his military arose within his heart, tempting David to honor himself and the power of the army instead of the Lord who had really given him the triumphant victories over the surrounding nations. The entire honor belonged to the Lord and His power of deliverance, not to David and the power of his military.

As soon as David issued the order, our Hidden Hero, Joab, challenged the census. Tactfully, Joab attempted to show the king his rebellion by both reminding him of God's power in his life and expressing a desire that the Lord would multiply David's troops. He questioned why David wanted a census taken. Without giving an answer, David overruled the objection of Joab and insisted that the census be taken. But the Scripture says, "Pride goes before destruction, a haughty spirit before a fall" (Prov. 16:18).

When David resolved to number the people, Joab tried to dissuade him from his purpose. Unsuccessful in his attempt to keep the king from this sin of pride, Joab performed the task slowly in hopes to give the king an opportunity to reconsider the matter.

He forgot for a moment that the strength of Israel did not consist in the number of its people but in the protecting care of God. Joab's statement and question to David would indicate this attitude from the king.

David's sin of pride would result in a three-day plague. Striking the entire nation, the plague took the lives of over seventy thousand people. Sin always takes you further than you want to go, costs more than you want to pay, and keeps you longer than you want to stay.

But the Lord showed mercy to the king. He was moved with compassion to stop the plague just as the angel was about to strike Jerusalem. This is the great message of this last chapter of the great book of Second Samuel. This chapter paints a dismal picture of sin and judgment but closes with the glorious theme of God's wonderful deliverance from sin and judgment.

Leadership Quiz: Is there leader hidden within your life today?

Are you willing to accept the responsibility to meet the challenges of this day?

Are you willing to be recognized for your accomplishments and attitude rather than your title or position?

Are you able to respect the authority God has placed in your life?

Are you willing to confront when you see a wrong that should be made right?

Are you a person whose reverence for God is the catalyst for the decisions in your life?

If so, then God is calling you to allow that hidden hero to hide no more. God needs men and women who have the gift of leadership. There is a city to take, a mountain to climb, a nation to win — and the call of God challenges all leaders to step forward. Remember this:

Leaders serve God faithfully.
Leaders discern God's vision for the day.
Leaders develop other leaders.
Leaders develop their spiritual relationship with God.
Leaders build God's community for His glory.

A Modern-Day Hidden Hero

He came into my office in Tulsa almost twenty-five years ago and said he was a freshman journalism major at a local college. He told me he had joined our church and wanted to see if he could be used some way in our ministry. I have learned now in over thirty years of ministry that when people walk into my office and volunteer to use their gifts and talents to honor the Lord, you immediately recognize their effort—almost invariably you discover that a Hidden Hero is standing before you.

Mike immediately took over the leadership of our church publications, and yet there was obviously more to this young man than just his journalistic ability. As I came to know him, I quickly realized his deep love for Christ and his global vision of reaching our world with the gospel. As a young man, not even out of college, he had already smuggled Bibles into countries behind the Iron Curtain. I witnessed his unreserved love for Christ in times of worship. In our denomination in the early eighties, anyone who lifted his hands in praise during worship either wanted to ask a question or was deemed a religious fanatic. Mike was the latter.

Sometime later, the Lord moved us to Florida, and I took with me the memories of a young Hidden Hero who was courageous in his convictions. You can only imagine my surprise when one day Mike once again walked into my office—only this time he was twelve hundred miles from home. Mike was now a college professor of journalism, in Florida to attend a conference. As we spoke together that day, Mike shared with me how he felt the Lord was calling him to ministry. However, what he said next has had a profound impact on my life, my family, and the ministry God entrusted to my care: "I believe God has called me to a very specific ministry. God has called me to serve you."

Talk about a humbling experience! Mike joined our ministerial team that year, and we have been together ever since. I have watched him grow in so many areas of his life, and yet I can say without reservation that God has used him so many times in my life that I could never adequately express my praise to the Lord for sending me this armor-bearer. Through the years, he has remained consistent in both his walk with Christ and the knowledge of his call. God knew I would desperately need a Joab throughout the years of my ministry.

Now, after almost twenty-five years, Mike continues to remain at my side, standing tall as a soldier of the cross and always there to support and encourage me in the ministry. Not long ago, Mike stood beside me as the assisting minister as we performed the marriage of my youngest daughter. He was right where he was supposed to be, at my side, standing for the good of my family and me. We give thanks to God for this Hidden Hero who as a young professional listened to the Father's call and came alongside.

CHAPTER 5

Huldah: Woman of Influence

If Jerusalem had awarded a "Woman of Influence" award in the days of King Josiah, it most assuredly would have gone to a woman that was not known for her philanthropic work but for her heart for God and her proclamation of the truth of His Word to His people. Prophets and prophetesses are not always the most popular people in the country, but they are the most vital people to any nation. This chapter's character is only mentioned in two verses of the entire Bible, yet her influence was evidenced in her brief appearance as our next Hidden Hero. Huldah the prophetess helped usher in a time of repentance and spiritual revival in the nation of Israel. Her influence was great even though her surroundings were meager. By examining Huldah's life, you can discover how you can be a person of spiritual influence in the world in which we live.

We already know part of Huldah's story, because she was a contemporary of Shaphan, the Hidden Hero who discovered the book of the law and brought it to King Josiah's attention. While Shaphan's story tells us much about the discovery of God's Word, the story of Huldah tells us about the application of God's Word.

Accomplished in the Word

After hearing the directives from the text of the newly discovered book of the law, King Josiah said to Shaphan and four other attendants:

> "Go and inquire of the LORD for me and for the people and for all Judah about what is written in this book that has been found. Great is the LORD's anger that burns against us because our fathers have not obeyed the words of this book; they have not acted in accordance with all that is written there concerning us." Hilkiah the priest, Ahikam, Acbor, Shaphan and Asaiah went to speak to the prophetess Huldah, who was the wife of Shallum son of Tikvah, the son of Harhas, keeper of the wardrobe. She lived in Jerusalem, in the Second District. (2 Kings 22:13–14)

Huldah was not a novice. She enjoyed a reputation as a prophet of God. To these men, among the top religious and governmental leaders of the day, she was already known as a prophetess. They "went to speak to the *prophetess* Huldah" (italics mine). How do we actually know she was accomplished in her profession as a prophetess? Look at the king's directive: "Go and inquire of the Lord for me and for the people and for all Judah about what is written in this book that has been found." Who do you go to when you are sick? A doctor. Who do you go to when your car needs to be repaired? A mechanic. Who do you go to when the king says "inquire of the Lord for me and for all the people what is written in this book..."? God's prophet. In this case it happens to be a woman of spiritual influence by the name of Huldah.

The Hebrew word for "inquire" is *darash,* which means to "diligently and thoroughly seek." When it was time to diligently and thoroughly seek the truth of God's Word, the highest officials in the land went to our Hidden Hero, Huldah.

Amazing as it may seem, it wasn't the priest or the other workers in the temple who had what the king needed most. In some cases, those who are professional in religious truth may not possess the true knowledge of God. In this case, it was a simple woman living in an impoverished area of the city, possessing the life of God in her soul, and she had more knowledge of divine truth than those whose office it was to explain and enforce the law.

That brings us to another significant reality in Huldah's life: She was poor. The writer of 2 Kings notes, "She lived in Jerusalem, in the Second District." It is not by accident that this scripture just happens to mention that Huldah lived in the "second district" in Jerusalem. This "second district" describes the outer portion of the city. King Manasseh had enclosed part of the extended city, to the north of the old city and near the city dump. It was obviously not the most desirable location to live. Why is this important for us to explore? It is important so we realize that some potentially great men and women of God have discounted the Word and work of God in their lives simply because of their circumstances in life. God puts no restrictions on the man or woman who desires to walk in truth. It didn't matter that she was poor or that she was a woman. God used her.

Huldah takes her place beside just two other godly prophetesses who were accomplished in delivering God's Word: Miriam (Exodus 15:20) and Deborah (Judges 4:4). Huldah's voice was heard as authoritative, able, and worthy to speak the words of God to very highest echelon in the kingdom of Judah.

Accessible to People

Huldah was available to God, but she was also accessible to God's people. The officials went directly to find Huldah. The indication is that she received the men, listened to their questions, and responded to them with the truth of God's Word.

This may seem like a trite point when talking about becoming a man or woman of spiritual influence, yet I would ask you, "Are you really accessible to the people God wants to speak to by using your life?" We are accessible for everything this world demands of us, but when it comes to the people of God we place our limits on what we will do. Honestly, what is more important, investing your time on the weekend watching a sporting event, or volunteering to touch, serve, and love the less fortunate? Could it be said of us that if the world "went to speak to us" we would be accessible to share the truth of God's Word, which has the power to change a life eternally?

Accountable to God

While she was one of the people and accessible to the people, Huldah also knew that the source of her wisdom was not her own strength, thought, or experience. When the king's men inquired of her, her response was immediate and certain: "This is what the LORD, the God of Israel, says..." (2 Kings 22:15). A true prophet of God understands that when speaking the Word of God, the prophet is accountable to the Lord for what is shared with others. Listen to what James says about accountability for teachers of the Word: "Not many of you should presume to be teachers, my brothers, because you know that we who teach will be judged more strictly" (James 3:1).

The religious leaders went to Huldah's home in part because they knew they would receive the truth without distortion, because she was accountable to God and took seriously her call to proclaim truth. Sadly, that is not always the case with every teacher of God's Word. Consider another observation from the New Testament, this one from the apostle Paul: "They want to be teachers of the law, but they do not know what they are talking about or what they so confidently affirm" (1 Tim. 1:7). It is a solemn moment when a person says, "This is what the Lord, the God of Israel, says..." At that moment you are directed to speak only the truth. You are not to add to the truth, and you must not take from the truth. Huldah was a tool in the hands of God, an instrument for revival, because she was accountable to God in speaking the truth of His Word to His people.

Authoritative in Proclamation

When the moment of truth came, Huldah spoke the Word of God with His authority, and she did not cover over the difficult aspects of this message. "She said to them, 'This is what the LORD, the God of Israel, says: Tell the man who sent you to me, 'This is what the LORD says: I am going to bring disaster on this place and its people, according to everything written in the book the king of Judah has read. Because they have forsaken me and burned incense to other gods and provoked me to anger by all the idols their hands have made, my anger will burn against this place and will not be quenched" (2 Kings 22:15–16). Notice this phrase: "Tell the man who sent you…" She is talking about the king of Judah. However, this woman of Godly influence has only one King, and His kingdom is not of this world. Even the greatest of people in this world, though gods to many, are nothing but mere created human beings.

For this earthly king, the message would be one of good news and bad news. First, the bad news: Destruction and bondage would come upon the rebellious people in Judah who had forsaken God. Next, the good news: The young King Josiah would be delivered from impending judgment, as a result of his repentant heart upon hearing the Word of God. As time would tell, Huldah's prophecy would be proven true in the subsequent events.

Accurate in Prophecy

The Bible reveals how to separate a true from false prophet: "You may say to yourselves, 'How can we know when a message has not been spoken by the LORD?' If what a prophet proclaims in the name of the Lord does not take place or come true, that is a message the LORD has not spoken. That prophet has spoken presumptuously. Do not be afraid of him" (Deut. 18:21–22). The records of the kings affirmed that Huldah's prophecy of doom and destruction would be realized in Judah. Two of Huldah's contemporaries, Jeremiah and Zephaniah, join her in this unfortunate vision of the future. Within four decades, the Babylonians would invade Judah. After twenty more years of war and subjection, Jerusalem itself would be destroyed and Solomon's temple would be dashed, stone upon stone.

Affirming in Grace

Despite this dire reality, Huldah knew that God sees the heart of the individual, even when a nation must be destroyed. She told the king's closest advisers, "Tell the king of Judah, who sent you to inquire of the LORD, 'This is what the LORD, the God of Israel, says concerning the words you heard: Because your heart was responsive and you humbled yourself before the LORD when you heard what I have spoken against this place and its people, that they would become accursed and laid waste, and because you tore your robes and wept in my presence, I have heard you,' declares the LORD. Therefore I will gather you to your fathers, and you will be buried in peace. Your eyes will not see all the disaster I am going to bring on this place.' So they took her answer back to the king" (2 Kings 22:18–20).

Notice that in her message from God to King Josiah, she shared some key spiritual truths for any of us today who desire revival or renewal in our life:

Rebellion is a reproach to God and leads to judgment.
Rediscovering the Word of God is essential to renewal.
Repenting of sin is essential if there is to be revival and
  restoration.
Receiving God's grace is the glorious evidence of revival.

King Josiah was told by this Hidden Hero that he would taste the grace of God. When he discovered the lost Word from the Father and realized his negligence, Josiah repented. God had seen his heart, and instead of judgment, peace would rule in the king's days. Today, this same directive will lead you to spiritual renewal, revival, and the joy of living in God's grace. The choice is yours. Five men went to this godly woman, Huldah, seeking a word from God. She spoke God's Word to this congregation of men, and her message was received, changing the heart of a king who in turn would lead a nation in revival and renewal.

A Modern-Day Hidden Hero

Tanna Dawson is a modern day Hidden Hero that you would recognize after mere moments in her presence. She was not born a woman of influence, but through a faithful life as a committed wife and partner of one of Florida's great spiritual leaders, she earned her reputation. Tanna and her husband were instrumental in being used by the Lord to rapidly spread the gospel in South Florida during a time when the East Coast Railway was just beginning to open up a new missionary field characterized by everglades, mangroves, and swampland. (This was long before spring break and sunny beaches!) Despite the real and uncertain shaky ground, Al and Tanna laid a solid foundation that has paced alongside the phenomenal growth of this area. Tanna's husband literally gave his life to seeing the gospel planted securely in that area. With his death decades ago, many thought Tanna would retire from active ministry and spend her remaining years enjoying some of the pleasures in life she and her husband had sacrificed for His work.

However, those who entertained that thought quickly realized it had no merit. Tanna remained in South Florida and redoubled her efforts, working tirelessly by looking for opportunities to encourage pastors, strengthening churches, and especially displaying her faithful and loyal support of her own local church. It would be impossible to begin to enumerate the contributions of this Hidden Hero, this precious woman who began in humility and continued to be clothed with this garment throughout her life. Most people who have buildings named after them receive that recognition because of their personal financial contribution or that of a family member. Not Tanna. The Tanna Dawson Center in Fort Lauderdale was named for this Hidden Hero because it was obvious to everyone that her life had been invested in those who most needed to know the promise of the Word of God. Now well into the twilight of her life, Tanna continues to be an ordinary woman who continues to produce extraordinary results as she quietly and faithful serves the Savior she loves. She's a true Hidden Hero of our day.

CHAPTER 6

Mephibosheth: Transformed by Grace

※

Look at this passage of Scripture:

> David asked, "Is there anyone still left of the house of Saul to whom I can show kindness for Jonathan's sake?" Now there was a servant of Saul's household named Ziba. They called him to appear before David, and the king said to him, "Are you Ziba?" "Your servant," he replied. The king asked, "Is there no one still left of the house of Saul to whom I can show God's kindness?" Ziba answered the king, "There is still a son of Jonathan; he is crippled in both feet." "Where is he?" the king asked. Ziba answered, "He is at the house of Makir son of Ammiel in Lo Debar."
>
> So King David had him brought from Lo Debar, from the house of Makir son of Ammiel. When Mephibosheth son of Jonathan, the son of Saul, came to David, he bowed down to pay him honor. David said, "Mephibosheth!" "Your servant," he replied. "Don't be afraid," David said to him, "for I will surely

show you kindness for the sake of your father Jonathan. I will restore to you all the land that belonged to your grandfather Saul, and you will always eat at my table." Mephibosheth bowed down and said, "What is your servant, that you should notice a dead dog like me?"

Then the king summoned Ziba, Saul's servant, and said to him, "I have given your master's grandson everything that belonged to Saul and his family. You and your sons and your servants are to farm the land for him and bring in the crops, so that your master's grandson may be provided for. And Mephibosheth, grandson of your master, will always eat at my table." (Now Ziba had fifteen sons and twenty servants.) Then Ziba said to the king, "Your servant will do whatever my lord the king commands his servant to do." So Mephibosheth ate at David's table like one of the king's sons. Mephibosheth had a young son named Mica, and all the members of Ziba's household were servants of Mephibosheth. And Mephibosheth lived in Jerusalem, because he always ate at the king's table, and he was crippled in both feet. (2 Sam. 9:1–13)

This Hidden Hero will teach us yet another lesson. However, this chapter's Hidden Hero will teach us not by what he did but by what he received. His name is Mephibosheth, and his story is the most beautiful picture of the doctrine of grace that you will find in all the Old Testament. This experience with Mephibosheth and his interaction with David shows the king at his very best. It is one of the most loving, tender, and gracious scenes in David's life. It involved a great act of compassion by David on behalf of Mephibosheth, the only son of Jonathan. We know that David and Jonathan were the best of friends. Jonathan was the principled son of an unprincipled king by the name of Saul.

Jonathan had been killed in war along with Saul when Mephibosheth was only five years old.

A number of years had passed since Jonathan's death when the events of this chapter take place. Mephibosheth now has a child of his own. However, David had not forgotten Jonathan's friendship and proved it, through an unselfish act of kindness toward Jonathan's son. It is in this encounter with King David that we see the doctrine of grace beautifully communicated.

David's Compassion

Do you wonder what caused David to ask the question in the first place? Was it the memory of his time of friendship with Jonathan? Regrets about the way his friend's end had come? Whatever it was, David wanted to know: "Is there anyone still left of the house of Saul to whom I can show kindness for Jonathan's sake?" Among his servants was one who had also served Saul. The servant, named Ziba, was called to David, who asked, "Are you Ziba?" "Your servant," Ziba replied. Then David asked his question again: "Is there no one still left of the house of Saul to whom I can show God's kindness?" Ziba, perhaps remembering the times his new king had been so kind even in the most impossible circumstances, replied, "There is still a son of Jonathan; he is crippled in both feet" (2 Sam. 9:1–3).

Ziba had been close enough to the circumstances years before to know David was a man of great compassion. Perhaps he knew this because even his own life had been spared, although as the conquering king David would have been justified in vanquishing the former king's entire court. Though David was a great warrior, he still maintained his compassion. He was a man of much emotion and feeling. His heart was a tender heart, and that is revealed in his compassion for Mephibosheth.

Notice three distinct aspects of David's compassion for Mephibosheth as these relate to the compassion our Savior has for each of us. First, David offers a compassionate investigation. He asks, "Who's left from the house of Saul?" When you read this chapter you may be quick to ask, "Why had the kingdom of Saul so fallen into obscurity and ruin?" The answer: Sin. The wickedness and rebellion of Saul brought his rejection and judgment by God. David gives a vivid description of people who are filled with sin and refuse to follow God: "I have seen a wicked and ruthless man flourishing like a green tree in its native soil, but he soon passed away and was no more; though I looked for him, he could not be found" (Ps. 37:35–36).

When David inquires "Is there yet any that is left of the house of Saul?" these tragic words emphasize the destructive power sin has on anyone who rebels against God. Sin destroys. It ruins. It brings the greatest to ruin. It turns beauty into ugliness, fruitfulness into barrenness, and life into death. Every age is filled with significant illustrations of this truth. It is my prayer that David's words, "is there yet any that is left…" would warn us of the great loss that can come to any one of us should we rebel against God and continue to live in sin. This compassionate investigation reveals the fall of Saul, but the king's compassionate investigation also reveals the faithfulness of David.

In 1 Sam. 18:3, about twenty years earlier, David made a covenant with Jonathan, his close and dear friend. It was a covenant of lasting friendship. David never forgot this covenant. He was faithful to what he had promised. And we should not forget our obligations. We cannot allow an atmosphere of prosperity and popularity to destroy our character or diminish our commitment to our faith and to the people we love. David's loyalty and faithfulness to this covenant also foreshadows our future with Christ and the compassion Jesus has for the world.

The compassion of Christ is seen in two different patterns in this love David shares for Mephibosheth. First, we see the scope of Christ's compassion. David wanted to show kindness to "any" member of Saul's family. None were excluded. In like manner, Christ will show eternal kindness to "whosoever," as revealed in John 3:16, and "Everyone who calls on the name of the Lord," as revealed in Rom. 10:13. In addition to the scope of Christ's compassion, we see the strength of that compassion. The compassion behind David's investigation was not a passing mood, but it was so strong that two decades had not diminished it. The compassion of Christ is even stronger. He had the strength of compassion that enabled Him to go to the cross for us.

In addition to this compassionate investigation, David offered a compassionate intention. Remember the tone of David's inquiry. "David asked, "Is there anyone still left of the house of Saul to whom I can show kindness for Jonathan's sake?" The intention of this compassion was found in the key word "kindness" (vv. 1, 3, 7). The Hebrew word for kindness is *hesed*, literally meaning "divine favor, absolute beauty, merciful." This is what the whole chapter is about. The specific intent of the "kindness" which David wanted to show is the "kindness of God." This was the specific kindness that was mentioned in the covenant between Jonathan and David.

This intention leads David to a compassionate inspiration, a bright idea that would forever illuminate the ways of grace. There is no question as to what inspired David's compassion to show kindness to "any" of Saul's family. The compassionate inspiration for Mephibosheth came as David remembered his love and covenant friendship with Jonathan. Apart from Jonathan, Mephibosheth would not have received this great kindness from David. Saul had tried many times to kill David, and when David was crowned king in Hebron, Saul's son Ishbosheth tried to maintain Saul's throne and wrest the crown from David. But because of his loyal covenant friendship with Jonathan, David was inspired to show kindness to "any" of the house of Saul in spite of the unworthiness of that house.

How beautifully this pictures the gospel of Christ. Like Saul's house, there is absolutely nothing in the sinner's life that makes him worthy of salvation. But because the Father thinks of His Son and remembers the covenant of love made possible by the blood of Christ, we have God's grace, His lovingkindness (*hesed*) as a result of the merit of Jesus Christ. Only because of that kindness can we have eternal life.

Mephibosheth's Condition

When the king discovers someone from the house of Saul, he's not who you might expect. Mephibosheth, grandson of one of Israel's once-great kings, has been permanently injured in both feet. The crippled condition of Mephibosheth is significant, because it parallels the condition of the sinner. Look at the amazing comparison of the condition of Mephibosheth to our condition as sinners apart from grace:

His Lineage: Mephibosheth was, of course, of the house of Saul. This was not the desirable lineage of that hour. The house of Saul was alienated from David. Saul had tried more than twenty times to kill David. Mephibosheth came from a house that was by character the enemy of David. As David ended Mephibosheth's alienation that was caused by his lineage, so Christ can end the sinner's alienation from God. Man is rejected from blessing because of sin. Tragically, the sin nature is in our spiritual lineage. We see our first tragic condition, our sinful lineage.

His Limp: The earliest description of Mephibosheth reveals he was lame. "There is still a son of Jonathan; he is crippled in both feet." How he became lame is reported earlier in the book of 2 Samuel: "Jonathan son of Saul had a son who was lame in both feet. He was five years old when the news about Saul and Jonathan came from Jezreel. His nurse picked him up and fled, but as she hurried to leave, he fell and became crippled. His name was Mephibosheth" (2 Sam. 4:4).

Notice how the crippled life of Mephibosheth also parallels

our life spiritually. He was injured when he was a young boy. This reminds us that from early in life, our crippled sinful nature is evident. In fact, the crippled heart of sin shows up even earlier in life than did Mephibosheth's lameness. We are born crippled. "'There is no one righteous, not even one'...all have sinned and fall short of the glory of God" (Rom. 3: 1i, 23). There is not a speck of goodness in any man apart from Christ.

Mephibosheth's lameness resulted from a fall. The crippled life of sin also is a result of man's fall in the garden. It was by Adam's fall that sin was introduced into our life and crippled our hearts. Being lame, Mephibosheth could not walk. He was hindered from living a full life. This would take great joy out of his life and prevent him from participating in many activities. So it is with the sinner apart from Christ.

This crippled life of Mephibosheth also emphasizes the doctrine of grace regarding our salvation. His lame life reminds us we cannot work our way to God's favor. We cannot do the works of God ourselves. We cannot walk in God's righteousness alone. It takes the King to bring us to His presence and make us whole.

His Location: "Where is he?" The king wanted to know immediately, and the servant Ziba responded that Mephibosheth was in place called Lo Debar. Lo Debar was distant and desolate. The meaning of the Hebrew word *lo-debar* is "waste" and means "a place of desolateness." This certainly describes the spiritual condition of those who do not know Christ. Mephibosheth's location in Lo-debar also speaks of the great distance he was from David, from the house of the king. Remember, being crippled, it would have been impossible for Mephibosheth to get from his place of distant desolation to the king's palace unless the king went to get him. Ephesians says the same thing about us: "But now in Christ Jesus you who once were far away have been brought near through the blood of Christ" (Eph. 2:13). David did for Mephibosheth exactly what Christ will do for us.

The Call of Mephibosheth

When the investigation of David had resulted in learning about Mephibosheth, David immediately arranged for a "call" to be delivered to Mephibosheth to come to David in Jerusalem. Note the following: Mephibosheth's call originated with the king. Our coming to Christ begins when we realize He is the one seeking us, not us seeking Him. Jesus stated this truth when He said, "The Son of man came to seek and to save what was lost" (Luke 19:10). Mephibosheth's call was a call of separation. David extended love to Mephibosheth, and his call would separate him out of desolation and into the dignity of the king's presence. David sent the servants to bring Mephibosheth "out of" Lo-debar to the king's palace in the presence of David in Jerusalem, where the conditions were much better.

Mephibosheth's call was delivered by the king's servant. Today, servants of God continue to take the call of God's grace to the desolate lives of those we know and invite them to a new life. Finally, Mephibosheth's call was a personal call from the king. When Mephibosheth arrived and prostrated himself before David, the first thing David said was "Mephibosheth." It was just one word, but it spoke great volumes. It was filled with great sentiment. By calling Mephibosheth by name, David sent a message of peace and reconciliation and love.

We see this in other cases in Scripture. When Moses turned aside to consider the burning bush, the first words he heard from God were, "Moses! Moses!" (Ex. 3:4). When Jesus looked up at the tree and saw Zacchaeus, His first word was "Zacchaeus" (Luke 19:5). It only took Chirst's tender calling of her name—"Mary"—to open the eyes of Mary Magdalene to the identity of the resurrected Christ near the tomb. And when Paul met Christ on the way to Damascus, Christ said, "Saul, Saul." Christ is the Great Shepherd, and "he calls his own sheep by name" (John 10:3). Salvation is not a sterile, cold, formal experience. It is a wonderful, heartwarming, delightful, and very personal experience.

The Change in Mephibosheth

Next, David said to the son of his friend, "Don't be afraid, for I will surely show you kindness for the sake of your father Jonathan. I will restore to you all the land that belonged to your grandfather Saul, and you will always eat at my table." One must wonder what Mephibosheth expected to hear. Did he wonder if David had been looking for whoever might be left from the house of his enemy Saul? Was he looking to eliminate the last of the line? Mephibosheth was surely amazed when instead of judgment at the king's throne he found more than mercy—he found grace. Significant changes took place in the life of Mephibosheth as a result of his response to the call of King David.

There was no more panic. "Don't be afraid," David said to him…" The great fear Mephibosheth would have had was death. Perhaps he thought, "Someday the king will find me, and my life will be over." He lived in fear his entire life that David would find him and kill him, and now he discovered that everything he thought he knew about David was a lie. The lie had filled his life with panic, but no longer.

There is peace. What peace would flood over Mephibosheth's heart when David said, "Fear not." All those years he was in Lo-debar, fear would be a constant companion. But now peace was his, just as peace is ours when we come to Jesus Christ!

There is a change in his position. Mephibosheth had a place at David's feasting table "just like one of the king's sons." Instead of a forgotten and disgraced fugitive in Lo-debar, he would now be treated royally, the same as any one of David's sons.

There is a change in his provisions. Four times we are told Mephibosheth will eat at the king's table. Provisions from the king included not only the necessities of life but also the fellowship with the king and with the king's family. The provision included the restoration of his entire inheritance, even the servants such as Ziba. In one moment, this man went from poverty to plenty.

There is a change in protection. Today people are concerned about their security—except when it comes to their soul security. They buy insurance to provide security to cover every event and aspect of their life, for their entire lifetime. David provided Mephibosheth with royal security. This tells us that David's kindness to Mephibosheth was not a temporary arrangement but a permanent one.

The great security provided to Mephibosheth was forcefully driven home in an incident that happened some years later. A famine came to Israel as a result of the mistreatment of the Gibeonites by King Saul many years earlier. David, after inquiring of the Lord as to the cause of the famine, asked the Gibeonites, "What shall I do for you? How shall I make amends so that you will bless the LORD's inheritance?" (2 Sam. 21:3). The Gibeonites wanted all of Saul's household put to death. This would have included Mephibosheth, who now sat at the king's own table. But the king "spared Mephibosheth son of Jonathan, the son of Saul, because of the oath before the LORD between David and Jonathan son of Saul" (2 Sam. 21:7).

The gift of God is enduring and everlasting. Even when the enemy attacks, God's salvation is sure. Mephibosheth tells the beautiful picture of the doctrine of God's grace and speaks of the security of every believer. Once a person comes to Jesus Christ for salvation, he is eternally saved. And just as Mephibosheth's sparing was not because of the goodness of his conduct but because of David, so the security of the believer is not based on the behavior of the believer but on God. Salvation is all about grace. No Hidden Hero illustrates the truth of God's grace better than Mephibosheth does.

A Modern-Day Hidden Hero

From the world's perspective, he was no impoverished Mephibosheth. If anything, he was the exact opposite of this chapter's Hidden Hero. About the only thing Mephibosheth and Bill had in common is they were both Jewish…and both crippled. Mephibosheth was crippled by accident. Billy (my name for my friend) was crippled by sin. Yet both, through the grace of God and the power of Christ, became Hidden Heroes.

I met Billy when our family joined his family in a "Welcome to South Florida" dinner. I was so looking forward to this dinner. I have been a New York Yankee fan since I was old enough to read the box scores and find out how Mantle did at the plate the day before. Billy is a limited partner in this most prestigious sports franchise in the history of sports, an owner of these legendary New York Yankees. As we spoke that night, the Lord knit our hearts together as friends, and I am forever thankful God brought him into my life.

That evening, Billy shared with us how God had found him, crippled in sin, left alone in his own spiritual LoDebar, and restored him and gave him a new life, living in the presence of King Jesus.

At a young age, fresh out of college, married with two young children, Billy's life appeared to be set, building upon the life work of his own father and mother in the world's most famous city. He owned one of New York's best restaurants. GQ magazine featured him in a three-page article. Yet the riches of the world began to blind this young man. Tragically, Billy came face to face with the consequences of living an impoverished life of sin. There were drugs, riotous living, women, alcohol, and gambling. Before long the bright lights of the fast life dimmed as he lost his wife and his children. Even in the separation, Billy failed to realize the poverty of his sinful life—until one day he had lunch with his estranged wife and she shared with him how she had been introduced to the Messiah. He walked away from that lunch infuriated that he had been told he was living a life condemned to hell.

Not long after, Billy's love for baseball would lead him to spend an afternoon with one of the Yankees' all-time greatest second basemen, Bobby Richardson. Bobby shared the story of Jesus with Billy, and suddenly this man of privilege realized he was bound in spiritual poverty. A few months later, Billy trusted Christ, and with the newfound faith of a child he asked God to deliver him from the bondage of cocaine and restore his family.

Today, Billy feasts regularly on spiritual delights at the king's table. He and his wife, Vicki, have shared their testimony of tragedy to triumph all over the nation. His is a perfect picture of a life crippled by sin and made right by God's great salvation. His impact and potential as a Hidden Hero is enormous. Billy is more than a Hidden Hero to me; he's one of my best friends, and I love him.[21]

CHAPTER 7

Ebed-Melech: Servant of the King

~~~~~~

Through the centuries, poets (who make their living waxing poetically) have extolled the high virtues of friendship. Yet friendship remains one of the most elusive relationships. We have acquaintances. Many of us have spouses. Some of us have children. But true friends? Much more of a challenge.

Want even more of a challenge? Search out the secrets of our next Hidden Hero, Ebed-Melech, and his role in one of the great friendships of ancient Israel. Ebed-Melech will teach us much about the principle of friendship, even though we have no evidence that Ebed-Melech even knew Jeremiah or was a friend to the king. The beauty of this story is simple; if Ebed-Melech would show this type of kindness and friendship to a total stranger in need, how much more should we share that friendship with one another?

Jeremiah had prophesied the destruction of Jerusalem because of the rebellion of the people for so long that he was thought of as a traitor. The Babylonian siege against the city had started and Jeremiah again shared God's Word of repentance or judgment. The men in King Zedekiah's court heard this message and ran to tell the king that the prophet was a traitor and was demoralizing the troops. He deserved to die, they said. The king abdicated any moral judgment and allowed Jeremiah to be thrown into a well that had no water but was filled with mud. As the prophet sank into the mud, it appeared he was left there to die.

At this point we are introduced to our Hidden Hero, Ebed-Melech. This man was from Ethiopia. He was a Gentile, not a Jew, and a servant of the king—a eunuch in charge of the king's harem. He was a man of administrative skill and obviously respected in the king's circle. Ebed-Melech was not really his name but a reference to his job; the name Ebed-Melech means "servant of the king." This man heard of the plight of Jeremiah and left his job to go to the city gate where the king was holding court. He boldly spoke on behalf of one who could not speak for himself.

Let's examine the background of this Hidden Hero in the text of Jeremiah 38:7–13:

> But Ebed-Melech, a Cushite, an official in the royal palace, heard that they had put Jeremiah into the cistern. While the king was sitting in the Benjamin Gate, Ebed-Melech went out of the palace and said to him, 'My lord the king, these men have acted wickedly in all they have done to Jeremiah the prophet. They have thrown him into a cistern, where he will starve to death when there is no longer any bread in the city.' Then the king commanded Ebed-Melech the Cushite, 'Take thirty men from here with you and lift Jeremiah the prophet out of the cistern before he dies.' So Ebed-Melech took the men with him and went to a room under the treasury in the palace. He took some old rags and worn-out clothes from there and let them down with ropes to Jeremiah in the cistern. Ebed-

Melech the Cushite said to Jeremiah, 'Put these old rags and worn-out clothes under your arms to pad the ropes.' Jeremiah did so, and they pulled him up with the ropes and lifted him out of the cistern. And Jeremiah remained in the courtyard of the guard. (Jer. 38:7–13)

Just as Jesus asked nearly a thousand years later, "Who is my neighbor?" Jeremiah surely must have been wondering, "Who is my friend?" In this stranger who became a true friend, the prophet would find his answer. Let's examine together the characteristics found in a true friend.

Conviction (verses 7–9): By the way this portion reads we know that while the king was making legal decisions and judging cases, Ebed-Melech left his own area of responsibility and interrupted the king on behalf of Jeremiah. This friend went above and beyond, beyond even his own well-being in order to stand on a principle of conviction regarding the injustice and inhumanity that this prophet of God had experienced.

Do you have a friend with this type of conviction? One who will stand for you or with you when they identify an injustice, regardless of what the majority may think? Does your church have people with this kind of conviction? Will we befriend those who, like the prophet Jeremiah, cannot speak for themselves? When we see an injustice done, will we stand? I believe God the Father waits and looks for those who will make a difference and act on their convictions. Today, we live in a nation of individuals in need of friends who will take a stand and speak up. It doesn't matter whether we stand up for the rights of the unborn or we continue to battle racism in our nation. When we see an injustice, are we the friends with conviction to make a difference?

Most likely, many people walked by the pit and heard Jeremiah cry out for help. There were probably several different responses:

The Sensitive Friend: "I feel for you down there, Jerry."

The Reflective Friend: "It is perfectly logical that someone would fall into that pit."

The Aesthetic Friend: "Perhaps I can share some ides that would help make that pit livable."

The Judgmental Friend: "So what did you do that caused you to be in the pit?"

The Analytical Friend: "Could you help me measure the depth of your pit?"

The Curious Friend: "Tell me, how did you first fall into the pit?"

The Perfectionist Friend: "Your imperfections caused you to deserve the pit."

The Self-Pitying Friend: "You think you have it bad—you should see my pit!"

The Meditative Friend: "Relax, breathe deeply, close your eyes, and don't think about your pit."

The Optimistic Friend: "Cheer up—you could have had snakes in your pit."

The Pessimistic Friend: "I think you'll eventually have snakes in your pit."

The Ebed-Melech Friend: "My lord the king, these men have acted wickedly in all they have done to Jeremiah the prophet. They have thrown him into a cistern, where he will starve to death when there is no longer any bread in the city."

Compassion: In addition to conviction, a true friend has genuine compassion. Consider again the story from Jeremiah: "My lord the king, these men have acted wickedly in all they have done to Jeremiah the prophet. They have thrown him into a cistern, where he will starve to death when there is no longer any bread in the city." It takes compassion to be a liberator and emancipator. Jeremiah was in a position of helplessness. He would die without a friend. The motivation for the friendship Ebed-Melech had for Jeremiah was the fact that he was moved with compassion; there was a man in need who would die without intervention.

This is the same kind of compassion Jesus displayed when He sat on the Mount of Olives and wept over the city of Jerusalem. He was moved in the depths of His being as He agonized over those in need.

A real friend will hurt when you hurt. Solomon said, "A friend loves at all times, and a brother is born for adversity" (Prov. 17:17). Here is a good test of your compassion as a friend. Think of those you are closest to, the people you call "friend"—do they hurt when you hurt? Now turn that test on yourself: When they hurt, do you hurt? Charles Spurgeon said, "A true friend is never known until the time of great crisis. From the fire comes a friend; guard that friendship with your life."

The text reveals the extent of Ebed-Melech's care and compassoin. He knows that Jeremiah is fatigued, famined, and fragile. Even the ropes intended for his rescue could cut and further injure Jeremiah. Ebed-Melech gathered rags to serve as padding that would act as a cushion to protect his arms.

There is nothing more important than to know you have a friend who will stand with you in the midst of your greatest pain and hurt. Frankly, at that point in life it doesn't matter who's right and who's wrong. But it does matter that you have a friend who cares about you, who loves you, and who will pray with you and for you.

Your friends are not going to be perfect. They will make mistakes, but so will you. Sometimes they will make stupid mistakes. At that time in their lives, they need a loyal and compassionate friend. This doesn't mean you endorse their behavior, but it does mean they know you will always be there.

That kind of friendship is not easy. Sometimes, it means you'll be cast out right along with the one cast out. Compassion may cost you, just as conviction will challenge you. That's why friendship must be marked with courage.

Courage: On the road to compassion, Ebed-Melech risks everything for his friend. He leaves his job and he goes to the king. But he doesn't just go to the king in private quarters. He goes to the king while he is at the most public of places, the city gate, listening to the citizenry and passing judgment. In front of everyone, Ebed-Melech courageously confronts the situation. He exposes the evil plot of those who attempted to silence Jeremiah and encourages the king to reverse his order and do what is right. A true friend will say what needs to be said, even if what needs to be said may hurt. In this case, Ebed-Melech was being a friend to the king as much as he was to Jeremiah.

Don't you wonder why the king responded so quickly to Ebed-Melech's request? The reason a true friend can say what's needed is that you know the heart of the true friend; that has been tested and proven true. Ebed-Melech had faithfully served the king. He had been entrusted with the king's most precious domain, his family. Ebed-Melech had invested much in the king's well-being. When the time came for his servant-friend to speak forthrightly, the king knew the words could be trusted. Ebed-Melech didn't pull any punches. He had the courage to tell the king that what the men had done to Jeremiah was wrong and that what the king had allowed to be done to the prophet was equally wrong. You want a friend with the courage to speak the truth in love.

Sometimes, even if you have the conviction, compassion and courage, you still need something else to be a friend: cooperation.

Cooperation: Did you notice the king's instructions to Ebed-Melech? He told him, "Take thirty men from here with you and lift Jeremiah the prophet out of the cistern before he dies." Great friendships are built on a spirit of great cooperation. A friend knows it is very dangerous to isolate yourself, and no true friend builds walls to keep other friends out. For Ebed-Melech, a partnership became essential. He found thirty men who would help pull Jeremiah from the well. Those thirty men represent a cooperative effort, a partnership that would provide both power and protection in the midst of a crisis.

Perhaps this cooperative effort—with Ebed-Melech, his king, the thirty men, and their newfound comrade Jeremiah—became the basis of an even greater friendship among all those involved. If so, we can be sure these friends of Ebed-Melech were walking models of conviction, compassion, courage, and cooperation.

A Modern-Day Hidden Hero

Some say that leaders are born in adversity. Sometimes the hidden leader has always been there, but it's the adversity in life that allows them to move from the ordinary individual to the extraordinary leader, the type of leader that I call a Hidden Hero. My friend Bill Hinson, known to his friends as "BH2," is this type of leader. Bill grew up in South Florida. His father is one of the most respected spiritual leaders in our nation and is a former pastor of First Baptist Church of Fort Lauderdale, the same church I've pastored since 1994.

When his father took a new position in another city, Bill remained behind in Fort Lauderdale, now as a young professional, married, and starting his career. Bill is the type of "preacher's kid" that every preacher prays his children will become. He has remained faithful to his Savior and deeply loves the local church. As a pastor's son, he has a unique insight into the life of a pastor and has the greatest respect for the undershepherd of God's people. As I have watched Bill through the years, I have become more and more convinced that whatever Dr. Bill and Bettye Hinson did in preparing the spiritual foundation for their children ought to be packaged and sold to every Christian parent. BH2 has been the model of consistency and spiritual maturity for all the years I have had the privilege of serving this great church. However, I never realized the strength of this man until I faced some days of adversity.

Bill was elected to serve as chairman of our deacons. In accepting the chairman's position, he realized both the honor and the tremendous responsibility he faced. Our church was in transition. Some of the leaders in our fellowship did not like the transition and were not supportive of my leadership. It was a difficult time for all of us, including those who opposed me. Looking back on that time, I now realize that God was using this opposition to refine my personal spiritual life and to develop an absolute dependence upon Him. In light of this great truth, I can now honestly say that I have no animosity toward those who stood in opposition to me. I believe they absolutely believed their position to be right. God used this opposition to spiritually refine me and develop strength for the ministry.

Having said all that, I will tell you that BH2's first meeting as leader of our deacon ministry was one of the most difficult meetings in which I have ever participated. In the midst of this tension, a leader was born. Bill held tightly to the Word of God and graciously listened to everyone's position. He diligently walked our church through what could have become a "spiritual shipwreck"; he was the perfect picture of strength. Often people look at those who are meek and make the tragic mistake of confusing meekness for weakness. The impact of the strength of Bill Hinson's leadership may not be known this side of heaven.

However, this much I do know about BH2. I know a pastor, who in the darkest moment of his entire three-decade ministry, found himself sitting at home with his wife in a totally dark house, weeping and feeling as if he could not live another day. Suddenly, the phone rang, the answering machine picked up, and in tears I heard this broken voice of a strong leader and friend, "Pastor, this is BH2. I know you are in your house, and I know you are hurting. I just want you to know that I am outside in your driveway. I too am hurting, and I want you to know I love you and I'm praying for you. Pastor, please don't give up. I'll be here if you need me."

Hidden Heroes seem to be born for the moment. At that moment, these ordinary individuals accomplish extraordinary feats. Ebed-Melech was a friend to God's man in his darkest hour. Jeremiah never forgot Ebed-Melech, and I will never forget Bill Hinson.

CHAPTER 8

Araunah: When Little Becomes Much

A llow me to tell you an amazing story about a problem, a proposition, and a provision. The problem came about because of success: the success of Jesus and His ministry. Everywhere He went, Jesus drew huge crowds. The crowds were so large that Jesus and His disciples didn't even have an opportunity to eat (Mark 6:31). They had been "peopled" to death. So Jesus and His disciples took a boat and crossed the sea to Bethsaida, hoping to rest their tired bodies and lift their spirits.

Have you ever noticed that when you think things can't get worse, they seem to get worse? Now here comes another problem: Some of the people saw the direction in which the boat went. "But many who saw them leaving recognized them and ran on foot from all the towns and got there ahead of them" (Mark 6:33). As the boat headed north, the crowd figured out that Jesus and His disciples were going to Bethsaida. So the masses took off on foot and were waiting to welcome Jesus and company when they arrive on the Bethsaida shore. So much for the hot tub, steak dinner, and a long weekend!

When Jesus saw the crowd, "He had compassion on them,

because they were like sheep without a shepherd" (Mark 6:34). The word "compassion" tells us that He sensed the needs of each person in that crowd. Five thousand men, plus women and children, gathered around Jesus as He taught, and He knew the spirits, the hopes, the dreams, the disappointments, the hearts of each one.

What a day! Jesus and the disciples were already tired when they arrived at Bethsaida and then they ministered that entire day. So as the shadows began to lengthen, Jesus drew His disciples aside, taking them a little farther up the slope to discuss the situation. There was a problem. Jesus summed up the problem in a question He put to the disciples: "When Jesus looked up and saw a great crowd coming toward him, he said to Philip, 'Where shall we buy bread for these people to eat?'" (John 6:5).

Jesus saw the problem and then gave the disciples an opportunity to devise a solution. In the midst of difficult times, we must remember that our problems are nothing but platforms for God to work a miracle. "He asked this only to test him, for he already had in mind what he was going to do" (John 6:6). In the disciples' responses, we will see reflections of ourselves. Many of us would have answered like Philip, the pragmatist. Philip answered him, "Eight months' wages would not buy enough bread for each one to have a bite!" (John 6:7).

Philip did not answer our Lord's question but offered statistics: 200 denarii would not be enough to feed the crowd. His answer revealed his problem—he was a bean counter. He had a calculator for a brain. Now I am not saying we do not need to be practical people. Every family needs a practical person, and so does every church. But Philip was the type of individual who decides everything based on figures and not on faith.

So now that we know the problem, where's the proposition? That's where another disciple, Andrew, comes in. Andrew spoke up with an idea: "Here is a boy with five small barley loaves and two small fish, but how far will they go among so many?" (John

6:9) On the surface Andrew's response appears to be an improvement, at least until he let his "but" get in the way. (He sounds just like his older brother Simon Peter! Must run in the family....) Andrew started out right, but he finished his proposition with a qualifier.

Andrew was like most of us. We want to believe God can do anything, but we also want to give Him an out if He doesn't come through for us. We want to protect His reputation! In doing so, we diminish the great possibility in the proposition: the possibility of faith in Christ and the trust in His power to provide. Had he fully understood the potential in Christ, Andrew might have said, "Hey, kid, let me borrow your lunch. You'll be amazed at what Jesus will do with it!" But instead he could not look past the limited resources he had in his hand.

Have you ever considered that Jesus did no miracle until something was given? The basic elements, the essential ingredients, the stuff of which hopes are made? Andrew simply looked at the resources in the proposition and decided there was no way to solve the problem. The disciples had terribly underestimated their wealth, and they sadly underestimated what God can do when a true sacrifice is offered to Him. They thought all they had was five loaves and two fish. What was wrong with them? They had been with the Lord. They had seen water changed into wine. The disciples had an incomplete view of Christ. This is very often the root of our problem, and quite frankly it is why so many of our spiritual propositions fail. They fail because we never understand that every problem, every proposition, every possibility needs a Provider.

The provision for the disciples came in a miraculous display of Christ's power. This was the most public of all of His miracles, recorded in all four Gospels, and in many ways it was the greatest. Mark 6:39 says, "Then Jesus directed them to have all the people sit down in groups on the green grass." It probably took some time to get them to do that. Then our Lord did something absolutely outrageous—He prayed and gave thanks for what He had...not for what He did not have! Can you imagine asking God's blessing on the food when there was no food? I imagine that some kept their eyes open, thinking, "What in the world is going on here?"

Then the unthinkable happened. Jesus took the loaves, gave thanks, and distributed to those who were seated as much as they wanted. He did the same with the fish. Verse 12 tells us that the crowd ate until they were all filled. This was not just a snack. There was so much food that the disciples gathered twelve baskets full of leftovers, enough for the next day. God takes care of those who serve Him.

Interestingly, the barley loaves the boy gave to Jesus were considered "poor man's bread," the cheapest of all breads. It's the same matzah bread that Jewish people use today when they celebrate Seder. In the Seder ceremony, celebrants read this from the Haggadah: "This is the bread of poverty. This bread which our ancestors ate in the land of Egypt, let anyone who is hungry come and partake. Let anyone who is needy, come and share..."

In our church, we have dozens of people who grew up in the islands of the West Indies: places like Jamaica, Cuba, St. Lucia. Those who come from this part of the Caribbean know exactly what I'm talking about. Their earliest childhood memories often include the aroma of an outdoor kitchen and a mother or grandmother faithfully making her own version of "poor man's bread," passed down from generation to generation.

Why would Christ use this food? He wanted His disciples to see that no matter what they had—even the tiniest or most menial thing—if they gave it to Him, He could use it. Even the "bread of poverty." The classic Christian hymn from the Depression era captures this principle with a simple but powerful phrase: "Little is much when God is in it." Jesus wanted the disciples to see this truth in a most dramatic demonstration. The problem was met with a proposition that resulted in a provision. The provision brought great honor to

Araunah: When Little Becomes Much

the Lord and blessing to the people.

So who's the Hidden Hero? Andrew? The little boy who gave up his lunch? The fish? No....none of these. Instead, let's turn our page back a thousand years and examine a similar heroic act, on a hill not so far away.

In the chronicles of Israel's royalty, we read about the greatest of all Judean kings, David. Also a great military commander, David one day reflects on his most recent triumph when an idea comes into his head. (The Bible says he was "incited" to this idea; in 1 Chronicles, the inspiration for the idea comes from Satan.) No matter where the idea came from—David's pride, Satan's scheme, or a combination of both—it turned out to be a terrible military misstep. David's idea was to count his fighting men, to take a census of all those who were eligible to serve in his armed exploits.

Scholars have debated why the census was so sinful, but David's chief military adviser Joab gives the answer: ""May the LORD multiply his troops a hundred times over. My lord the king, are they not all my lord's subjects? Why does my lord want to do this? Why should he bring guilt on Israel?" (1 Chron. 21:3). In other words, it didn't matter how many fighting men David had. Even if he had only a small number, God would multiply their efforts a hundred times over. Joab understood this principle: that little is much, even when it comes to the strength of an army, when trusted to the hands of the Lord. David, on the other hand, seems to have forgotten the lesson he had learned as a boy when he allowed six little stones to be much in the hands of God. Joab challenges the wisdom of David's order, but David stubbornly insists that he carry it out anyway. The military leaders start their nine-month census, finding more than a million soldiers in Judah and Israel.

So here was David's problem in a nutshell. It's similar to the kind of problem many men and women deal with today. It is a problem that, unlike the problem with Jesus and the multitude, was not a result of success but of sin. David, having conquered the surrounding enemies in obedience to God, lacked something positive to do, so he decided that he would enlist his military leader, Joab to take a census of all the eligible men in Israel who would qualify for his army. Joab (another one of our Hidden Heroes) confronted David and encouraged him not to take this action, even reminding him that it is the Lord who has delivered the enemy into the king's hands, but pride often overtakes powerful people and David fell prey to an even more formidable enemy.

In one sense, it is ironic that it was actually success that caused this problem. David failed to attribute his success to God's power and provision. It is a frightening thought that your blessing could become your burden if you fail to maintain your spiritual perspective. God never ignores our sin and shortcomings. He never looks the other way, never makes excuses, and never winks. He'll forgive when He sees genuine repentance, but if not, He'll judge the sin until He sees brokenness and humility.

We find David in the process of being judged for his sin. The Lord gave him three options: three years of famine, three months of being chased by the enemy, or three days of plague. David chose door number three, and the plague began. Seventy thousand people died. David cried out to the Lord when he saw the pain he had brought on innocent people. That is an aspect of sin that the enemy never reveals until it is too late. God moved mercifully in the heart of David and led him to a threshing floor north of Jerusalem for an encounter with the angel who is administering the plague.

In the midst of his problem, David did what every one of us should do when we feel the discipline of the Lord. He acknowledged the problem. The problem was pride, and the problem was the sin of David and David alone. "When David saw the angel who was striking down the people, he said to the LORD, 'I am the one who has sinned and done wrong. These are but sheep. What have they done?' " (2 Sam. 24:17). God hears David's cry and sends to him a prophet of mercy, the same one who had pronounced the choice of three penalties for the census. The prophet says: "Go up and build an altar to the LORD on the threshing floor of Araunah the Jebusite" (2 Sam. 24:18).

Ah! Enter our Hidden Hero! David knew the territory of this threshing floor well....it's the same place he had just encountered the angel and pleaded for the plagues to cease. Let's pick up the conversation between these two men, David and our Hidden Hero, Araunah:

> So David went up, as the LORD had commanded through Gad. When Araunah looked and saw the king and his men coming toward him, he went out and bowed down before the king with his face to the ground.
> Araunah said, "Why has my lord the king come to his servant?" "To buy your threshing floor," David answered, "so I can build an altar to the LORD, that the plague on the people may be stopped."
> Araunah said to David, "Let my lord the king take whatever pleases him and offer it up. Here are oxen for the burnt offering, and here are threshing sledges and ox yokes for the wood. O king, Araunah gives all this to the king." Araunah also said to him, "May the LORD your God accept you."
> But the king replied to Araunah, "No, I insist on paying you for it. I will not sacrifice to the LORD my God burnt offerings that cost me nothing." So David bought the threshing floor and the oxen and paid fifty shekels of silver for them. David built an altar to the LORD there and sacrificed burnt offerings and fellowship offerings. Then the LORD answered prayer in behalf of the land, and the plague on Israel was stopped. (2 Sam. 24:19–25)

What do we know about Araunah? He was a wealthy Jebusite farmer who owned private property in the area we would later call Jerusalem. He sold his threshing floor to David as a site for an altar to Jehovah, together with his oxen. It doesn't sound like a big deal, yet we will learn much from this simple but obedient farmer. From this situation we are now introduced to the proposition.

Look again at the historical account: "So David went up, as the LORD had commanded through Gad. When Araunah looked and saw the king and his men coming toward him, he went out and bowed down before the king with his face to the ground. Araunah said, 'Why has my lord the king come to his servant?' 'To buy your threshing floor,' David answered, 'so I can build an altar to the LORD, that the plague on the people may be stopped'" (verses 19–21).

The proposition is simple. David needs to atone for the sin that has brought this devastation upon his people, and God tells him to build an altar using Araunah's property. The only problem with this proposition is it involves Araunah's willingness to surrender what he had in his control. This is a magnificent picture of stewardship and sacrificial giving. Araunah will be faced with these questions: Do I sacrificially give, knowing that it will not bring an immediate benefit to me? Do I sacrificially give, knowing that it will appear on the surface that I am burdening my profit-loss statement? Or do I have the faith to sacrificially give in obedience to God's directive in this proposition and trust Him with taking care of my needs?

Our Hidden Hero made all the right decisions in this proposition.

I want you to fully understand in this picture of stewardship what Araunah actually gave to King David:

Respect: "When Araunah looked and saw the king and his men coming toward him, he went out and bowed down before the king with his face to the ground. Araunah said, 'Why has my lord the king come to his servant?' " (verses 20–21). How important was this act of respect to this broken king at this time in his life! I believe the actions of Araunah served as a reminder of David's sin and his failure to exhibit the same respect for the King of Kings who had so faithfully cared for his every need. Araunah immediately establishes the proper respect in identifying the obvious: I am the servant, and you are the king.

Friendship: In responding to David in this manner Araunah revealed that he chose not to further condemn the king for his sin but to be a friend and help assist him in whatever way possible. It is my desire that God would give us more Hidden Heroes like Araunah.

Generosity: Araunah offered the king not just what he asked for but also much more. The king asked for a piece of land. Araunah offered the land, the oxen to be sacrificed, and the wood with which to build the fire. "Araunah said to David, 'Let my lord the king take whatever pleases him and offer it up. Here are oxen for the burnt offering, and here are threshing sledges and ox yokes for the wood. O king, *Araunah gives all this to the king*'" (verses 22–23, italics mine).

Witness: More than simply give the elements for the altar, an even greater gift that our Hidden Hero gave to the king was a witness of stewardship and trust. "Araunah also said to him, 'May the LORD your God accept you'" (verse 23). In responding in this manner our Hidden Hero demonstrated his love for the king and, more importantly, his love and faith in the Lord. He was willing to give the property to the king and offer his prayers for the king's offering to be given to the Lord. Here is a key principle: In Araunah's mind, once the gift was given, the altar and the offering would have been David's completely, because he had transferred the stewardship to David. In this line of thinking, David then would have the decision to build on his property the altar and to sacrifice his oxen to the Lord. What a heart of a man who understands the principle of stewardship!

Now we examine the final aspect of the victory that was

made possible by our Hidden Hero, and that is the provision extended by God. David, in an act of obedience, realized a very vital truth in the example of Araunah. Those who have tasted the mercy of God understand that our motivation for worship is centered on His grace. Araunah demonstrated grace in offering his riches, and now David would understand the significance of the sacrifice. David's provisions were seen in the altar of sacrifice and the sacrifice on the altar. On the altar of sacrifice, blood was shed, and the fiery judgment of God was stopped.

Have you ever considered that the manner in which you worship is a tremendous indicator of how you view God's grace in your life? David would not consider a cheap religion that cost him nothing. Both David and Araunah gave of their best on this day of worship. God help us if we resort to cheap worship and have churches filled with worshippers who have failed to understand the significance of God's sacrifice for us.

Do you know how we know that the spirit of cooperation between Araunah and David worked together for God that day? "David built an altar to the Lord there and sacrificed burnt offerings and fellowship offerings. Then the LORD answered prayer in behalf of the land, and the plague on Israel was stopped" (verse 25). The Lord answered the prayer and received the sacrifice, and the grace of God replaced the judgment of God. The confirmation from that altar of worship was evidenced in these ways:

>   Prayer was answered
>   The price was paid
>   The sacrifice was accepted
>   Grace was received
>   God was honored
>   God's people rejoiced

A man by the name of Araunah was willing to give everything...just like the little boy who gave his lunch. For

Araunah, it wasn't lunch, but a piece of property. But have you ever wondered what became of that little piece of land?

One wonders if, in the days before biblical archaeology and informative documentaries on the History Channel, Araunah could have known the significance of the threshing floor on which he and David stood. The land Araunah sold to David that day was the exact same land where Abraham had walked his son Isaac to the top of the hill, prepared to offer him to the Lord as an act of obedience. When God saw the heart of obedience He stopped the knife and provided His own offering to take the place of Abraham's son.

It was this same mountain where Isaac's son, Abraham's grandson—Jacob—would stop for rest and awake from a visitation from the Lord and proclaim, "How awesome is this place! This is none other than the house of God; this is the gate of heaven" (Gen. 28:17). Now eight hundred years later, God once again is receiving a sacrifice, and once again God's grace is demonstrated. On this land offered by Araunah, David built a temporary altar. A few years later, David's son Solomon would build the Temple of God—God's very dwelling place on earth, with the Holy of Holies and the Ark of the Covenant—on that very same spot (2 Chron. 3:1). In fact, the very name of the mountain—Mount Moriah—means literally "chosen by God."

However, the story doesn't stop there. Travel with me a thousand years later. Now, on this same piece of land known as Moriah, we see Roman soldiers taking the King of Kings to this hill and nailing him to a cross. We watch the offering, the offering that cost God the Father everything, being placed on the altar. The sacrifice is accepted for the sin of mankind. For those who by faith have trusted Christ, the judgment of God stops at the cross on Calvary, at the foot of Mount Moriah, and relationship with God is renewed and restored forever.

It all began with a man named Araunah, who had given what he could. Little became much—more than we could ever imagine—as that small piece of property became the very land on which our Savior would offer His life. In his classic book *The Temple Mount,* Solomon Steckoll writes, "There is an outcropping of starkly bare rough limestone rock in Jerusalem which for thirty centuries past has gripped the minds and hearts of sons of men as being the most sacred spot on earth. Known to the Jews as the Temple Mount and to the Moslems as the Noble Sanctuary...few places in the world have been...as sacred as this city, this flattened mountain and this rock. While the world lasts and as long as the sons of men believe that one spot on it is more sacred and hallowed than another, this will remain so."[22]

Another Jewish historian, Josephus, recorded that after David built his altar and "saw that God had heard his prayer, and had graciously accepted his sacrifice, he resolved to call that entire place The Altar of All People." And one day, according to the book of Revelation, on that same mountain, a great multitude of "all people" will gather again—just like that crowd of five thousand, except a crowd so great that no one will be able to count it. They'll be "from every nation, every tribe, people and language." And they'll be "standing before the throne" of the temple, "in front of the Lamb" who was sacrificed, crying out in a loud voice, "Salvation belongs to our God, who sits on the throne, and to the Lamb" (Rev. 7:9–10). Angels will fall down on their faces and worship God, saying, "Amen! Praise and glory and wisdom and thanks and honor and power and strength be to our God for ever and ever. Amen!" (Rev. 7:12).

What are you holding in your hand today that you feel is not worthy to offer to Him? Little becomes much when it is placed in the Master's hand.

A Modern-Day Hidden Hero

Dave was not born into a privileged family. As a matter of fact, he didn't even have much of a family at all. He was

Araunah: When Little Becomes Much

adopted when he was four, but his adoptive mother died before he was a teenager. His adoptive father remarried and moved often from town to town looking for work. About the only stability in his life came from his Grandmother Sinclair.

Having been told by his father that he wouldn't make it in the world, Dave dropped out of school and went to work in a restaurant. Later he would take those skills into the military and work in the kitchen while serving his nation. God did bring goodness into his life when he met and fell in love and later married his childhood sweetheart. Dave and Lorraine began their life partnership, a partnership that would have greater acclaim than anyone might imagine. He opened his first restaurant in Columbus, Ohio, and named it after his daughter. He started the business on these principles:

Great service: Treat everyone with respect, regardless of who they are or whatever their background.

Great product: "Never cut corners," he would say. That, by the way, is why his hamburgers were square, not round... because he didn't cut corners.

Fair price: Don't worry about becoming rich, but be concerned that everyone "gets a piece of the pie."

I met Dave in the twilight of his career. We became good friends. Dave amazed me. He was one of the brightest men I have ever met and yet one of the most unassuming men this world has known. He truly valued people. He and his wife never forgot their roots, and they become known as two of America's most generous philanthropists. Thousands of children are in homes of their own today because of the focus Dave put on adoption and because of the foundation he established. (The I. Lorraine Thomas Children's Emergency Home and Family Support Center is part of his lasting legacy and love for these children and his wife.)

Those who know me well certainly know that I do not say this lightly: I loved Dave Thomas. He was one of the greatest men I have ever met, and in my short five years with him before his passing, I learned so much about life, about people, and about myself. Obviously, the founder of Wendy's was not "hidden." After all, everyone remembers Dave and his commercials. What has been hidden is this hero's story of how God can take little and do so much if just one man will yield his life to Him.

CHAPTER 9

Bezaleel: Gifted Child of God

※

All over the world, people are asking questions like these:

"What am I living for?"
"What is the purpose of all this?"
"Am I making a difference?"

For many, these questions are quickly met by feelings of emptiness and loneliness, a sense of helplessness, disappointment, depression, and even despair and hopelessness. Many people find themselves trapped in an endless cycle of futility. They live a life where nothing lasts, at least not for long. Tragically, they fear that at the end of their life on earth they will find virtually nothing of significance.

Thoreau was right when he wrote from Walden Pond, "The mass of men lead lives of quiet desperation. What is called resignation is confirmed desperation. From the desperate city you go into the desperate country... A stereotyped but unconscious despair is concealed even under what are called the games and amusements of mankind." Thoreau continues, "When we consider what, to use the words of the catechism, is the chief end of man, and what are the true necessaries and means of life, it appears as if men had deliberately chosen the common mode of living because they preferred it to any other. Yet they honestly think there is no choice left."[23]

This is not so for those of us who are in Christ, and the catechism's directive to which Thoreau refers is the only choice worth making: "The chief end of man is to love God and enjoy Him forever." Every Christian believer who follows Christ understands that obedience brings purpose, meaning, and significance. God has gifted all believers and stirs their hearts to serve Him. When we serve God, we experience a deep, rich fulfillment; when we serve God, the Father gives us spiritual satisfaction, spiritual significance, and spiritual security.

Consider the biblical story of this chapter's Hidden Hero, an obscure construction worker named Bezaleel:

Then the LORD said to Moses, "See, I have chosen Bezaleel son of Uri, the son of Hur, of the tribe of Judah, and I have filled him with the Spirit of God, with skill, ability and knowledge in all kinds of crafts—to make artistic designs for work in gold, silver and bronze, to cut and set stones, to work in wood, and to engage in all kinds of craftsmanship. Moreover, I have appointed Oholiab son of Ahisamach, of the tribe of Dan, to help him. Also I have given skill to all the craftsmen to make everything I have commanded you: the Tent of Meeting, the ark of the Testimony with the atonement cover on it, and all the other furnishings of the tent—the table and its articles, the pure gold lampstand and all its accessories, the altar of incense, the altar of burnt offering and all its utensils, the basin with its stand—and also the woven garments, both the sacred garments for Aaron the priest and the garments for his sons when they serve as priests, and the anointing oil and fragrant incense for the Holy Place. They are to make them just as I commanded you." (Exod. 31:1–11)

Bezaleel perfectly portrays the personal joy of the gifted child of God who understands both the fact that he has been empowered by God and enjoys the fellowship of living in obedience to God's direction in his life. We will see his service and the wonderful results of his obedience and have a living example of this Hidden Hero, who directs us on being a "gifted child" our Father would be proud of in this world.

There are four key principles regarding our service that we will glean from this Hidden Hero: our commission to serve, our capability to serve, our cooperation in service, and our command to serve. God's commission on Bezaleel's life is forthright and firm: "See, I have chosen Bezaleel," He says to Moses. Then Moses tells everyone else, only a few chapters later: "See, the LORD has chosen Bezaleel" (Exod. 35:30). God Himself appointed Bezaleel to be superintendent of the construction. The name Bezaleel means "under the shadow of God," or under God's protection and guidance.

The picture of our Hidden Hero is graphic: God had been protecting and guiding Bezaleel throughout his life as an Egyptian slave. God protected him from injury and prepared him in spite of the circumstances. Perhaps even because of the circumstances, Bezaleel was uniquely ready to serve as construction coordinator, combining his own skill and ingenuity with what he had observed from his Egyptian masters. There are times that we have great difficulty seeing any good or even any God in our days of bondage, strife, failure, and difficulty. Yet we must remember that God sees our life in detail while we see it only in the day. What is the Father using in your life today to prepare you for service that will result in His glory tomorrow?

When we consider the commissioning of God on our lives, let's begin with this biblical premise: Every believer is called by the Father and commissioned to serve in some way. "Each one should use whatever gift he has received to serve others, faithfully administering God's grace in various forms," according to 1 Pet. 4:10. Peter, the apostle who had seen it all, would have known that this was a significant change from the older ways. How did the Lord commission His work in Old Testament times? When there was an important job to be done, God chose a person to do it, and the Spirit gave that person the ability, the experience, and the power to complete the task. The Spirit gave our Hidden Hero, Bezaleel, the ability to build beautiful and artistic structures. God gave Joab military wisdom! To King David, God gave the gift of leadership. In the life of the Huldah, the Father gave the gift of prophecy. In the Old Testament, the Spirit came upon individuals in order to accomplish specific goals at a specific time. In the New Testament, God's approach had changed, and Peter was there to see it. As the Spirit came upon all believers at Pentecost, they were empowered to do God's will and fulfill His purpose for the new church. This probably wasn't so much a change from the way God worked in the Old Testament, but the massive outpouring in one place at one time made His empowerment of these New Testament believers especially profound.

Remember, Christ has commissioned every believer to serve in the body. It may be serving by taking care of an infant in a church nursery or taking care of a senior adult in a nursing home. Service for the Lord is not always about being on the stage and performing. Bezaleel was not called to be a priest. He was not called to be a Levite and lead the worship. He was called to be a builder and use the gifts and talents the Lord had given him to make just as great an impact as a preacher or soloist.

Allow me to use our church's Fort Lauderdale Christmas Pageant to illustrate this point. For more than twenty years, God has used this ministry to share the news of Christ with literally millions of people, when you consider the live audiences and television viewers around the world. Even the world has recognized the uniqueness of this presentation; the pageant broadcast has been awarded two regional Emmys and numerous other awards. However, most of those who make the pageant happen (by God's power) serve either behind the stage or in front of the stage but not in the spotlight on the stage. But the commission is equally essential…the stage lights wouldn't go on without someone to flip the switch. Without the purposeful contribution of each commissioned believer, we'd all be in the dark.

God knew Bezaleel even when he was still in his mother's womb. Here's a thought for you to consider: The God of the universe, the Creator of all things, knew Bezaleel personally. The call of God is not an impersonal, faceless procedure. The commissioning of God goes right to the heart of individuals and sets them apart to serve God's people.

Once we comprehend the truth that God has called us to serve we must also have the knowledge He has equipped us to complete the service. As God is telling Moses all about His selection of Bezaleel, He hands Moses Bezaleel's impressive resume: "...and I have filled him with the Spirit of God, with skill, ability and knowledge in all kinds of crafts, to make artistic designs for work in gold, silver and bronze, to cut and set stones, to work in wood, and to engage in all kinds of craftsmanship."

As the tabernacle is being constructed, we have an excellent illustration of one who has received the spiritual, intellectual, and skillful capability to serve as overseer of this building project. Much artistic skill was required in making the tabernacle—God Himself was the architect—and God gave Bezaleel exacting skill and knowledge. Others besides Bezaleel were also endowed with these skills, but Bezaleel was the leader of these skilled men. God is still gifting His people and making them capable to serve Him in the body of Christ.

Please allow me to distinguish between the "gift of the Spirit" and the "gifts of the Spirit." One is singular and the other plural. Every believer is given the gift of the Holy Spirit to come and dwell inside. God's Spirit dwelling in you gives you the potential to change—not only to change your life but also to influence and change your community, through the privilege to use the power of God.

Look at Rom. 12:1–8:

Therefore, I urge you, brothers, in view of God's mercy, to offer your bodies as living sacrifices, holy and pleasing to God—this is your spiritual act of worship. Do not conform any longer to the pattern of this world, but be transformed by the renewing of your mind. Then you will be able to test and approve what God's will is—his good, pleasing and perfect will. For by the grace given me I say to every one of you: Do not think of yourself more highly than you ought, but rather think of yourself with sober judgment, in accordance with the measure of faith God has given you. Just as each of us has one body with many members, and these members do not all have the same function, so in Christ we who are many form one body, and each member belongs to all the others. We have different gifts, according to the grace given us. If a man's gift is prophesying, let him use it in proportion to his faith. If it is serving, let him serve; if it is teaching, let him teach; if it is encouraging, let him encourage; if it is contributing to the needs of others, let him give generously; if it is leadership, let him govern diligently; if it is showing mercy, let him do it cheerfully.

Notice what Paul says about spiritual gifts "We have different gifts, according to the specific grace and capability given to us." This means that the gifts are given to *believers*... after we come to know the grace of God. Every believer should pursue a program online, in a book, or in a church that will provide an education in the biblical description of spiritual gifts. Each should discover his or her own gifts and find ways to immediately serve in the body of Christ. In serving, believers will bring glory and honor to Christ, what I call "incarnational communication."

Incarnational communication is a term that speaks of the spiritual responsibility of every Christian, as modeled by Jesus Himself. Incarnation, which alone refers to the physical presence of Jesus among men, is derived from the Latin word "incarnatio," which means "taking on flesh." (Like one of the Latino delights in South Florida and Texas, chili con carne....chili with meat!) The most important incarnation came when God became man. While it is a biblical idea, it is not a biblical term. Christians began to use the word around 300 A.D. based on their study of John 1:14: "The Word became flesh and made his dwelling among us. We have seen his glory, the glory of the One and Only, who came from the Father, full of grace and truth." When we add the term "communication" to "incarnation," it becomes something totally different but wonderfully the same. When we allow His incarnational communication to work through us—because we have seen His glory—then we become reflections of that same glory, full of His grace and models of His truth.

As God's "gifted child," you will be capable of fulfilling any job the Spirit of God commissions you to complete. Often, however, people either ignore the call of God or refuse to use their God-given capabilities to honor the Lord and strengthen the body of Christ. We must be careful as God's gifted children that we do not fail to use the gift of God responsibly. Every believer should be permitted as far as possible to follow the bent or direction of his own giftedness, especially when the believer understands she is gifted by God for a purpose! I am amazed at the way our world looks and evaluates talented and gifted people. Some say, "He's a natural." Yet when you study stories from Scripture, you are humbled to remember, "I am not naturally gifted in anything, but supernaturally gifted by the great grace of God."

The apostle Paul, never one to give credit where credit isn't due, said this about our God-given capabilities: "Not that we are competent in ourselves to claim anything for ourselves, but our competence comes from God" (2 Cor. 3:5). Paul knew he was incapable of communicating or understanding the truths of the gospel. Paul wanted everyone to know that the truth he shared came from the Lord. He had no power of his own to reason or to convince men and women to turn from their sin and trust Christ. That was all of God. As a result of this understanding, he claimed no right to boast in the success of the ministry or in his strength. All success was to be traced to God. Paul's confidence was founded not on human reason but on his divine resource.

Paul is a tremendous example to all of us in Christ; he gave God the credit for all his accomplishments. At Corinth, the false teachers boasted of their own power and prestige, but Paul expressed his humility before God. No one is adequate in providing any ministry that has eternal significance without God's help. No one is competent to carry out the responsibilities of God's calling on his or her own strength. Without the Holy Spirit's enabling, natural talent can carry a person only so far. As servants in the body of Christ, we should all test our attitudes. We should ask ourselves this question: "When the ministry I participate in begins to succeed, who will get the credit: Christ or me?"

As gifted children of God, we have been commissioned to serve, and we are capable of serving. But if we don't cooperate with God's purpose and plan, this service is meaningless. Read through God's specifications to Moses again: "See, have chosen Bezaleel son of Uri, the son of Hur, of the tribe of Judah, and I have filled him with the Spirit of God, with skill, ability and knowledge in all kinds of crafts—to make artistic designs for work in gold, silver and bronze, to cut and set stones, to work in wood, and to engage in all kinds of craftsmanship. Moreover, I have appointed Oholiab son of Ahisamach, of the tribe of Dan, to help him. Also I have given skill to all the craftsmen to make everything I have commanded you." Here is the picture of cooperative effort using great workmanship directed by divine leadership.

Remember that the name 'Bezaleel' means in the "shadow of God"; even his name beautifully illustrates the ministry of the Holy Spirit. Like the Spirit, Bezaleel gave every man his work, and when every man did his job, the work was completed and done with excellence. God's method of operation is the same today. He still commissions us and gives us the gifts we need for our particular ministry.

Then He expects us to cooperate with one another to complete the task. Paul reminds us, "There are different kinds of gifts, but the same Spirit. There are different kinds of service, but the same Lord. There are different kinds of working, but the same God works all of them in all men" (1 Cor. 12:4–6). If we would each simply be faithful to our appointed tasks and cooperate together, can you imagine what God can accomplish? We will need this cooperative effort if we are to see the vision God has given to us become a reality.

The body of Christ is designed in a way to illustrate our absolute dependence upon Him and our cooperation with one another. The church is built to strengthen one another as we use our gifts and talents to honor Him. No one individual has every spiritual gift or talent. That is what makes the cooperative effort in service so very essential. This spirit of cooperation also illustrates the importance of us working together to both encourage one another and help one another in the difficult times. I often hear people who are not biblically literate speak as if they are speaking with knowledge say, "I can be a great Christian without being part of a church." The sad truth is this attitude violates a clear biblical directive. We are one body with many members. We need all parts of the body working together for us to be healthy and growing.

One of my longtime coworkers, Toni, is a minister on our staff team who specializes in assisting our members in determining their spiritual gifts, then placing them in a ministry which allows them to realize the best of what God has given them. The process is extensive and comprehensive, and the result is that people who want to serve God are able to do that in a way which is personally rewarding, intentionally challenging and good for the believer and good for the church. Toni's own life is a model of one believer, completely committed to the Lord, totally willing to unwrap the spiritual gifts He has given and see them deployed so the church can be the church it's intended to be.

Our church ministry team is built around such leaders who have searched God's Word and will to understand and develop their gifts. I think of Jeff, our minister for creative arts who worked his way through seminary with some of the nation's best dance companies. Jeff and his wife Christye are choreographers for the Fort Lauderdale Christmas Pageant, and he's one of the most thoughtful Bible scholars I know. I think of Brian, a legendary New York Yankee who serves our church as minister for outreach, and of Terry, who served as a high school baseball coach and joined our team to lead men's discipleship programs and our single adult ministry. Both men draw on their skills in sports and coaching for mentoring others. I think of Nathan, a former university administrator whose people skills form the foundation for our counseling ministries. I think of David, a former morning television news producer who leads our media ministries. I think of Nicole, my executive assistant who joined our team after successful careers in the nation's fastest-moving cities and lends organization and expertise to all our endeavors. Very few of our ministers started out as professional ministers, but God drew upon their unique abilities and experiences to call them. Denise, Marsha, Mary, Lynn, Julie, Sandi, Thaly, Rachel, Bill, Ron, Robin, John.....the list goes on as a wonderful portrait of the Father's plan for His family. That's one of the reasons these men and women are so intent on seeing our own church model what Paul taught.

Paul always set his discussion of gifts in the context of the church. This also repudiates those who tend to think only individualistically. When one person begins to focus only on his "gift," this leads to spiritual arrogance. "I have the gift of evangelism!" "My gift is taking care of babies in the nursery."

Paul spoke of gifts in terms of the whole church, not in terms of individuals. When Paul used the analogy of the body as it relates to the church, he reminded us that the body has many separate members, such as the eyes, ear, leg, or nose. Each member has a corresponding ability (to see, or hear, or walk, or smell). This understanding leaves no room for arrogance or shame concerning our gifts. In his writings, Paul referred to about twenty different spiritual gifts, which makes it obvious we need one another.

King Solomon understood this principle of spiritual cooperation in our service:

> Two are better than one,
>> because they have a good return for their work:
>
> If one falls down,
>> his friend can help him up.
>
> But pity the man who falls
>> and has no one to help him up!
>>
>> Also, if two lie down together, they will keep warm.
>>
>> But how can one keep warm alone?
>
> Though one may be overpowered,
>> two can defend themselves.
>>
>> A cord of three strands is not quickly broken.
>> (Eccles. 4:9–12)

Bezaleel took the "gifted children of God," organized them according to their talents and their passions, and completed the work that God assigned.

Finally, we recognize that the commissioned Bezaleel was committed enough to combine the capability he had received from God and the cooperation he received from others into a strong response to God's command in service. God was not inexact in His orders to Moses: "…They are to make them just as I commanded you." What is the significance in doing our work, "just as I commanded you"? The construction job under the direction of our Hidden Hero was amazingly successful.

The story of the building of the tabernacle is one of great spiritual significance and scientific magnificence. It was a building precise in every detail. Once the tabernacle was completed, it never again required attention, addition, or alteration. This temple was so carefully constructed that it endured half a millennium and fell only to repeated attempts at its literal destruction. No wonder God was so specific in the way He wanted it built! And no wonder He chose one who knew how to serve—this Hidden Hero—to be its builder.

A Modern-Day Hidden Hero

I have the privilege of working with one of the most gifted and creative ministerial teams in the nation. Their talent is without equal, and I am so honored to say the same can be said about the spiritual integrity of each team member. Great churches always have one constant and transferable concept in common…they are led by a great team. Through the years, I have been saddened to see how some church leaders have built their ministry totally around their own personality or strength of their charisma. It is sad and yet almost universally true that such churches and organizations are only as strong as their charismatic leader. As soon as he has the opportunity to move on to the next bright horizon, the fabric of his leadership and the foundation of his work becomes painfully obvious. In this type of leadership you won't necessarily find a Hidden Hero, because leaders like this have worked hard to make their greatness known everywhere.

I have come to believe that the greatest organizations, including God's church, is best served by a strong spiritual leader who understands the value of shared leadership. In this model, the spiritual leader will aggressively seek to build the strongest team possible and will build the organization around the true value of every member of the team. My two most enjoyable times in terms of team leadership have been in two Florida churches: Merritt Island and Fort Lauderdale. While I have loved every place the Father has given to me to serve, and while each church is unique and special in its own right, the most enjoyable times have come when we were able to assemble a team of people who shared the same values, the same convictions, and the same love for one another.

Many people speak of "building the team." Sadly, most of this talk is nothing but rhetoric intended to entice you to come and join them reach the goal of continuing to build the reputation of a man. Real teams understand each other's strengths and weaknesses, and they never assume a territorial position. Instead, like Bezaleel, they stand ready and equipped to serve wherever they are needed. When I look at our team, I see a real team with real skills, real talent, genuine love, great integrity, and a bond among themselves that cannot be broken.

Several years ago, the Father sent a young man named John into my life. He is one of the most gifted and godly men I have ever served with in ministry. In the past, I have had brothers speak to me in the same manner in which Jethro, the father-in-law of Moses, spoke to Moses. In love, they have reminded me that I cannot do everything. In my attempt to keep my hands on all the moving parts, I will lose effectiveness and be distracted from my real calling. I never fully comprehended the depth of that counsel until John joined our team and became one of the strongest leaders I have ever known. Even as I write this, I am mindful that I have the time to invest in writing this book because John is using his gifts of administration and relieving that pressure from my life. John is a modern-day Bezaleel. He is skilled and gifted, not only in the mechanics of administration but also in relationships with people and the kind of cooperation that keeps a church strong. He is filled with the Spirit of God and ready to be used in the service of the King. Another Hidden Hero is discovered.

CHAPTER 10

Eunice: Mother with a Mission

Think about one person in your life who has nurtured your faith in Jesus Christ. Many of you thought immediately of your mother. Moms and dads have an important role in nurturing the faith of the children entrusted to their care. Parents of faith realize God has given them a wonderful privilege. Those of us who have been nurtured by our moms in the faith understand that we have a legacy to create fresh opportunities to pass on that faith.

This Hidden Hero is a mother who understood this. Many mothers are heroes to their children, and every Christian mother is not just a hero but also a great gift from God to her family. But Eunice was a single mother in a scary world. She was a Jewish believer in Jesus. She'd been married to a Greek unbeliever who had either left or died. Like today, rearing a child in a single-parent home at that time was no picnic. As we follow the life of Eunice we can provide helpful guidance to parents and Christian workers who have a heart's desire to build the spiritual life of children.

Eunice, as a Jewish believer, would have been well-versed in these passages from the poetic books of the Old Testament: Psalm 139:13–14—"For you created my inmost being; you knit me together in my mother's womb. I praise you because I am fearfully and wonderfully made; your works are wonderful, I know that full well"; Psalm 127:3—"Sons are a heritage from the LORD, children a reward from him"; and Prov. 22:6—"Train a child in the way he should go, and when he is old he will not turn from it." From these passages, Eunice would know that her legacy would be found in the way she hid the hope of God in the hearts of her children. She accomplished this in three ways: education, example, and expectation.

The Education of Our Children

The first key principle is to educate or teach our children the things of the Lord. Paul instructed Christian parents to embrace the high calling of bringing up their children "in the training and instruction of the Lord" (Eph. 6:4). Timothy, one of the better-known heroes of the Bible, became especially useful to the Lord and to the apostle Paul in part because from childhood his mother, Eunice, and his grandmother, Lois, had instructed him in the Word of God. Paul even commended and challenged his young protégé in 2 Tim. 3:15 to remember "how from infancy you have known the holy Scriptures, which are able to make you wise for salvation through faith in Christ Jesus." This reminds me of my colleague Kevin, whose single-parent Mom raised him and his brothers in this very same way.

Where do parents get the blueprint for raising children with a solid biblical education that provides them the foundation for their future? This instruction was set forth early in Israel's history. God gave very specific instructions to His people related to the education of their children. He commanded them to personally and genuinely accept His truth with uncompromising conviction and devotion, and left clear instructions on how to educate their children in truth:

Eunice: Mother with a Mission

These are the commands, decrees and laws the LORD your God directed me to teach you to observe in the land that you are crossing the Jordan to possess, so that you, your children and their children after them may fear the LORD your God as long as you live by keeping all his decrees and commands that I give you, and so that you may enjoy long life. Hear, O Israel, and be careful to obey so that it may go well with you and that you may increase greatly in a land flowing with milk and honey, just as the LORD, the God of your fathers, promised you. Hear, O Israel: The LORD our God, the LORD is one. Love the LORD your God with all your heart and with all your soul and with all your strength. These commandments that I give you today are to be upon your hearts. Impress them on your children. Talk about them when you sit at home and when you walk along the road, when you lie down and when you get up. Tie them as symbols on your hands and bind them on your foreheads. Write them on the doorframes of your houses and on your gates. (Deut. 6:1–9).

In that passage, God gave ancient Israel a final warning not to forget Him and His Word after they had come into the Promised Land and were confronted with material blessings. Look at Deut. 6:12–14: "Be careful that you do not forget the LORD, who brought you out of Egypt, out of the land of slavery. Fear the LORD your God, serve him only and take your oaths in his name. Do not follow other gods, the gods of the peoples around you." Like their parents, our children need to beware that the culture in which we live offers many false idols that lure them away from the Lord. Eunice insured that the lure of the world would never overtake her son's love for the Lord by starting early to build a biblical foundation for his life.

Parents ask me how early we should begin to teach our

children the principles of our faith. I tell them, "From the moment you discover God has blessed your womb." Paul's challenge about "how from infancy you have known the holy Scriptures, which are able to make you wise for salvation through faith in Christ Jesus" speaks of anticipation. When a mother anticipates, prays, and leads her children toward Christ, she can expect the cooperation of God in bringing her child to the Lord. This sounds simple, but it doesn't come easily or cheaply. Susannah Wesley, the mother of some of the greatest men of God in the history of Christianity, is said to have prayed one hour every day for her children. She was strict. But she was unselfishly faithful. She had six rules for teaching her children the priority of the Savior:

1. Subdue self-will in a child.
2. Teach my children to pray as soon as they can speak.
3. Give my children nothing they cry for and only what is good for them when they ask politely.
4. Punish no fault confessed, but let no sinful act to go unnoticed.
5. Reward good behavior.
6. Strictly observe all promises you have made to your child.[24]

The Example of Our Lives

Susannah Wesley's rules demonstrate that education alone is not enough, especially if not illustrated in a daily example. Paul knew this, too, and commented on it in his letter to Timothy: "I have been reminded of your sincere faith, which first lived in your grandmother Lois and in your mother Eunice and, I am persuaded, now lives in you also" (2 Tim. 1:5). A second principle for building a spiritual foundation in the lives of our children focuses on the spiritual example of your own life. What legacy are you leaving your children by the example you are establishing before them today? Essentially we must remember more is *caught* in our homes than *taught*. You are the model of what you want your children to become.

Let's return to the verses we just read in Deuteronomy 6. It is clear from these instructions that God's Word was not simply to be taught to our children, but parents are instructed to teach the principles of our faith by their daily example in everyday life. God's Word and the principles we live by are to be illustrated in all we do. Please remember that the life of Jesus was just as inspired as the words of Jesus. The disciples learned by watching!

Just as the Israelites were to bind God's Word on their hands and foreheads and write it on their doorposts, so Christian parents can have Bible verses throughout their homes, play Christian music, let their children watch some of the excellent animated Christian videos, and find other creative ways to continually reinforce scriptural truths. What the Lord was teaching His people is a simple truth that educators teach even today. Our student minister, Ryan, reminds parents that children learn by principle and by picture. Some will learn more by visual teaching while others will gravitate to audio instruction.

As much as we are encouraged to provide these resources, parents can nullify the biblical teaching by inconsistent living. Godly parents will clarify and communicate God's Word in their children's minds, hearts, and lives as they watch their parents living out the truth of what they have taught. As a part of our example to our children we are called to provide living reminders of God's Word in action. We must also remember that the failure to honor these instructions carry pain just as obedience brings praise.

I want to illustrate this critical point with Scripture. Children not only need godly precepts but also require godly patterns from their parents. Consider the story of an Old Testament priest named Eli: "Now Eli, who was very old, heard about everything his sons were doing to all Israel and how they slept with the women who served at the entrance to the Tent of Meeting. So he said to them, 'Why do you do such things? I hear from all the people about these wicked deeds of yours' " (1 Samuel 2:22–23).

Eli should have known the answer to this question. While as a priest he was skilled in knowledge about God, he set the stage for immorality and infidelity among his sons by his own inconsistency. When Eli attempted to discipline his sons they ignored him, partly because he had not taken the time in the past to deal with their rebellion and partly because they had no respect for him due to his own compromised lifestyle.

Parents should never underestimate the importance of their own Christian example in the home. They must have a firm conviction that their walk with Christ is for their own spiritual maturity and obedience and not just for the sake of their children. Many young parents return to the church of their childhood because they want moral instruction for their own children, so they can have what they had. But a child's perceptive spirit will sense when a parent is manipulating them or when they see us acting in a manner different than our instruction. It is the authenticity of a parent's lifestyle commitment to live in obedience to truth that brings the freedom to share and to pass to the children we love.

Look at this premise statement for this vital principle in our homes: A spiritually mature motive for passing on truth as a parent to my children is that the truth I teach them is also essential truth for my daily life, independent of my children's response to the same truth.

Eunice is evidence of such a positive pattern. She's a second-generation believer. Timothy's a third-generation believer. All this in Christianity's infancy! Look at the verse, and you will identify that it is obvious that Lois came to Christ first and then led her daughter, Eunice, to Christ. Eunice then influenced her son Timothy: "I have been reminded of your sincere faith, which first lived in your grandmother Lois and in your mother Eunice and, I am persuaded, now lives in you also." We must never underestimate the life-changing potential of raising one small child to know the Word of God and to love the Lord with all his heart. It is imperative that you view every child God has given to you in trust as a potential Timothy.

A key principle in securing the spiritual foundation in the life of our children is rooted in the example of the physical, spiritual, and emotional embrace you provide for your children. We must love them with the same love that Christ has shown to us. At this point you are leading by example. Only parents who lovingly weep with their children, rejoice with them, hurt with them, give their time to them, show them genuine affection, and sacrifice for them will effectively influence them in the things of the Lord and will successfully build a spiritual foundation. If you won't live it, don't bother to teach it. They will learn what you live. A child who sees her mother carry a Bible to church but never open it from Monday to Saturday is educated to understand that Christianity is only for Sunday. Your example matters.

The Expectation of Our Hearts

The third and final principle given to us by this Hidden Hero is the wonderful expectation for God's leadership that Eunice displayed in rearing Timothy. After parents have done everything humanly possible to rear their children in the way of the Lord, they must ultimately trust Him to make those efforts fruitful. Only the Holy Spirit can reach into the human heart, including the heart of a child, and only His power can give spiritual life and empower spiritual faithfulness. Eunice had great expectations for her son and for God's work in his young life. Her expectation is evidenced even in the name she gave him. Timothy's name means "honored by God." At birth, this Hidden Hero was walking by faith and saying something like this: "Lord, I will do my part to lay the spiritual foundation in my son's life, and I am asking you to honor this commitment by using Timothy for your glory." I believe that what we expect God to do in the life of our children honors the Lord and gives a clear and consistent message to our children that they are young men and women of faith who will carry on the legacy of faith long after we are gone.

Eunice is a Hidden Hero because she was a godly mother who realized that the spiritual success of her family begins with her personal relationship with God. When we dedicate children at our church, we meet with the parents first and share with them the biblical responsibility they have to provide a spiritual foundation for their children. We also pray for the parents at the altar during the time of dedication. In fact, our preschool director Barbara makes sure parents are dedicated to the Lord before we dedicate their children. Some parents will mistakenly say to the church—not out loud, of course—"You train up my child in the ways of the Lord. I don't have time, and I don't want to get involved, but I know they need a Christian foundation." "Mother" and "father" are not honorary titles; they are working job descriptions.

How does these "great expectations" become reality in the life of your children? Expectations always require action, and the action is yours. First, introduce your child to the Savior. Second, instruct your child in the Scriptures. Third, inspire your children to service. Paul's observation about Eunice's expectations for her son? "So that the man of God may be thoroughly equipped for every good work" (2 Tim. 3:17).

Parents, you can't expect your child to know and grow in the Lord unless you know Him first. The greatest gift you can give your children next to their introduction to Christ is to be a real Hidden Hero in their lives because of the way you live, the way you love, and the way you lead. We need more Hidden Heroes in our homes. Eunice's name means "the victorious." What greater victory could a parent have than to know and see their children walk in the faith of our Lord and Savior?

A Modern-Day Hidden Hero

Without question or reservation, I would say that the one woman who most demonstrates the Hidden Hero qualities as witnessed in the life of Eunice is a woman in our church most affectionately known as Sandy. Paul wrote, "Likewise, teach the older women to be reverent in the way they live, not to be slanderers or addicted to much wine, but to teach what is good. Then they can train the younger women to love their husbands and children, to be self-controlled and pure, to be busy at home, to be kind, and to be subject to their husbands, so that no one will malign the word of God" (Titus 2:3–5).

Sandy is the modern-day model of the instructions Paul gave to the older women. We first met Sandy when we welcomed her into our home in Mobile, Alabama, for a visit. She was representing the pastoral search committee for First Baptist Church of Fort Lauderdale, and she was there to pray with us as we joined together seeking the perfect will of God. From the moment Cynthia and I met Sandy, we knew she was a woman filled with the Spirit of God. She was the real deal. Little did we realize that over the next decade, we would have the privilege of growing together with a true matriarch for our entire ministry. She was and continues to be the perfect example of a Proverbs 31 woman and a great model for every Christian woman who aspires to such a level of spiritual maturity. (I know a lot of people say that about women in their lives, but if you knew Sandy, you'd know that she's a supreme example of this passage.)

There has never been a ministry responsibility too small or too large for this woman. She is absolutely in love with Christ, and her love for the Lord is demonstrated in her commitment to His church. Others talk about the great Bible teachers they have been through the years, but give me Sandy any day…I'll always take the "walk" before the "talk"! What is amazing about this modern-day Eunice is that she excels in every area of her life. She is an incredible wife, she has reared three great children, and she is a blast to have for a grandmother. For more than two decades, she has been the coordinator for the single largest ministry in our church, the Fort Lauderdale Christmas Pageant, which is seen by fifty thousand people in person each year with television audiences of millions more. In addition to those major responsibilities, she also puts on her painter's pants and paints the walls, hangs pictures, redecorates furniture, plants the flower beds in the church, bakes the bread, hosts the guests, organizes the decor of the church facilities, and still has time to be one of the most influential women in South Florida. (She serves on several community-wide boards for nonprofit organizations and civic associations.)

I have prayed with Sandy, laughed with Sandy, wept with Sandy, and served with Sandy. She has my vote for the Hidden Hero who best demonstrates the qualities found in Eunice. Finally, if the Lord were to ever feel the need to write an addendum to Proverbs 31, He would have to say, "And by the way, follow the example of Sandy as she has so faithfully followed Me."

CHAPTER 11

Anna: Super Senior Saint

※

There was also a prophetess, Anna, the daughter of Phanuel, of the tribe of Asher. She was very old; she had lived with her husband seven years after her marriage, and then was a widow until she was eighty-four. She never left the temple but worshiped night and day, fasting and praying. Coming up to them at that very moment, she gave thanks to God and spoke about the child to all who were looking forward to the redemption of Jerusalem. (Luke 2:36–38)

In the prime of life, or so they say. Lost her husband at an age way too young, living a life without him way too long. Perhaps the young who passed by her would have said her usefulness had come and gone. Say she had married at sixteen, lived with her beloved for seven years as the Bible says, then lived on for eighty-four years after that. Even with such a conservative calculation, she likely would have been 107 years old. Now she stands in the temple, waiting for her turn, waiting for heaven's door to finally open. And open it does! Except it opens the other way, and she's right there when the Son of God steps into the world of man.

Anna was a woman who had grown old loving God with all her heart and all her mind and all her soul and all her strength. And after her days and years and decades of faithful service, she discovered like so many before her and so many since that God indeed does save the best for last.

Anna was from the tribe of Asher, the least important of all the tribes of Israel. Asher had come from the son of Jacob and Leah's maid, Zilpah. Leah was the unwanted wife, and Zilpah was the unwanted slave of the unwanted wife. Asher was the last and least of the four slave-born sons of Jacob. Yet Asher never allowed that status to bother him. His name means "happy." He made up for the deficiency of his birth with the joy and gladness of his disposition. Just because a person comes from humble circumstances doesn't mean he cannot be happy. Anna was born into the "happy tribe," and she seems to have acquired the two characteristics of that tribe: humility and happiness. However, this Hidden Hero added a third characteristic in her life: She was also holy!

This Anna is the godly old woman whose name is forever associated with the birth of the Lord Jesus Christ. She is the woman whom God allowed to see His Son when He was a tiny infant, a baby of just six or seven weeks old. She saw a little one who was dependent for every human need and upon the ministry of a mother. And Anna also realized this little one was the One on whom the entire world would depend.

Jesus had been circumcised when He was eight days old, and now after the appropriate lapse of time, Mary had now come to the temple with her holy child to offer the sacrifice demanded after a woman had given birth. A mother was required to bring a sacrifice to the temple forty days after the birth of a son. On this particular occasion God allowed Anna, our Hidden Hero, to hold His Son in her arms. As we explore the life of this "super senior saint" we will see within her a victory that transcends our limited time in this world, a vocation that makes those short years worthwhile, and a vision that extends long after we are gone.

The Victory of a Saint

In our study of Hidden Heroes, we often find very little is told about their lives. As a result, we must read between the lines of Scripture and history. When considering Anna, we know this about her life: When she was very young, she was married. She and her husband anticipated a wonderful life together, many children, grandchildren, a blessed home. Tragically, her husband died after only seven years of marriage, and she was left a widow. She could have become bitter. Few would blame her. We all know people who have turned bitter after the death of one they loved so much. They blame God for their sorrow. They speak rashly and accuse Him of cruelty. Satan wins a victory by distorting their perceptions of God.

Sadly, they don't realize that God is just as saddened by the curse of death, so much so that He allowed this One whom Anna held to overcome the eternal impact of death for all time. Still, in this temporal life, death still walks the earth invading every home, eventually breaking up every marriage, ripping open the hearts of parents who have lost a child, and turning this world into one giant cemetery. God is not the one to blame for death's visit, the rightful owner of that blame would be the sin of mankind. Too often, bitterness is part of the sin cycle that keeps us in bondage even though the promise of God is life.

Think for a moment about the choice Anna had to make. She could have easily been bitter the rest of her life, blaming God and hating anything to do with Him. If that were the case you would not find a happy old woman, but a bitter, sour woman whom few people liked. Consider this additional fact: With her husband dead, Anna probably had to work to make enough to survive. At harvest time, she would glean at the edge of the fields where the other poor were looking for food. She would come home to an empty house that would be silent yet haunted by promising but unfulfilled memories. Her life was so very, very difficult. However, Anna did not withdraw into bitterness and hatred. She did not live in discouragement and self-pity. Instead Anna turned to the Word of God and lived in the truth of God's Scripture. Perhaps she claimed this verse from Isaiah: "I will give you the treasures of darkness, riches stored in secret places, so that you may know that I am the LORD, the God of Israel, who summons you by name" (Isa. 45:3).

Anna learned to trust God for treasures in the midst of her darkness. So Anna entered into victory. She would make God's house her home, and God would be her husband. She would find in Him the fulfillment of her emotional longings as she considered the love of her life that was gone. She made God her husband, she made His house her home and her work, and she entered into the "treasures of darkness." In the temple courts, she found a quiet corner that became her real home. Luke tells us, "She never left the temple but worshiped night and day, fasting and praying." She could say with Job, "Though he slay me, yet will I hope in him; I will surely defend my ways to his face" (Job 13:15). Instead of becoming bitter at the tragic death of her husband, Anna dedicated her widowhood to God, and in the process she determined to be the happiest and holiest widow in Jerusalem.

So we have to ask: What was it in her life that enabled her to reject the bitterness of this defeat and live in victory? Once again we need to look a little deeper. Anna's father was named Phanuel, which means "the face of God." Anna had the benefit of being raised in a godly home and having the privilege of having a wonderful spiritual heritage. Anna grew up in a home where her father was a living image of God to her childish soul. She saw the face of God in the face of her father. She knew what God was like because she knew what her father was like.

My own father had his faults and failings like anyone else, but there were certainly times he showed me the face of God in his humble heart, his gentle smile, and his tenderness when he spoke of the things of the Lord in his later years. Why do so many Christian parents see their children go astray? Sometimes it is because the children look at their parents and do not see the face of God. Christian parents must do more than talk about what is right. Their supreme responsibility is to live Christ so that their children will think of the face of God whenever they think of their parents.

Even though Anna was not bitter over her family, she could have been bitter over her declining health. A person does not live to be more than a hundred years old without accumulating the inevitable physical consequences of old age. She could easily have excused herself from serving in the temple because of her old age and declining health. But Anna's desire and the absolute delight of her life was to be where God's people assembled. This is one saint who loved to be in church! Anna would have said, "I'm looking for the coming of the Lord, and when He comes I know where I want Him to find me. There are thousands of places where I don't want Him to find me. I know where I want Him to find me, and I know where I'm most likely to find Him, in the house of the Lord. You'll never keep me away from God's house and God's people."

It is important to study Luke 2:37: "She never left the temple but worshiped night and day, fasting and praying." The word "never" is strong word. There were no ifs, ands, or buts: Anna lived solely for the place where God had put His name. Her whole life revolved around the activity and service in the house of the Lord. A verse in Anna's Bible told her that the Lord would come suddenly into His temple: "See, I will send my messenger, who will prepare the way before me. Then suddenly the Lord you are seeking will come to his temple; the messenger of the covenant, whom you desire, will come," says the LORD Almighty" (Mal. 3:1). She did not know where else He would come, but she knew He would come there. So the temple was where Anna wanted to be.

She wanted to be there, no matter who else was there and no matter what her personal situation was or her level of distress. Someone like Anna could have been bitter over her lack of finances. Once again, she refused to use her lack of economic success as a reason to avoid going to the temple. Not only did she have limited resources of her own, but also she likely would have seen up close the religious charlatans who were interested in taking advantage of women just like her. Jesus spoke of those charlatans in Mark, perhaps inspired by the memory of innocents like Anna: "As he taught, Jesus said, 'Watch out for the teachers of the law. They like to walk around in flowing robes and be greeted in the marketplaces, and have the most important seats in the synagogues and the places of honor at banquets. They devour widows' houses and for a show make lengthy prayers. Such men will be punished most severely" (Mark 12:38–40).

Under Jewish law, a widow could not dispose of her property except through the rabbis, and it is obvious some were not honest. Quite possibly Anna herself had been cheated. But the fact that some people use religion as a cloak to cover up their wickedness made no difference to Anna. She was not going to let their hypocrisy rob her of her own joy in the Lord. She refused to live in the bitterness and the potential bondage of the past. Anna was able to conquer the everyday tragedies of life that cripple so many of us and cause us to live a life filled with bitterness. Instead, Anna found her victory in the Lord, and by yielding herself to Him she found His peace for her life.

The Vocation of a Saint

As we've seen, God's Word instructs us that this remarkable woman "never left the temple but worshiped night and day, fasting and praying." This is more than a sideline, a pastime, or a once-a-week visit for Sunday worship; Anna devoted her whole life to deepening her relationship with the Father and to the ministry of intercession and prayer. Her life was filled with one great anticipation and expectation—that she would see the Messiah!

It is interesting that when we read of Anna's work we see this little old woman, bent and feeble, doing what the high priest should have been doing. As we examine Anna's commitment, we see a tragic truth, a truth evident even in our day. Many of the ministers who served in the temple were more interested in gaining political power than being filled with priestly power. We also see this dear old woman doing what the Levites should have been doing. Anna's whole countenance brightens as she begins to allow the praise of the Lord to escape her lips. She never tired of praising the Lord and enjoyed her work so much that the scripture says she was in worship around the clock: "She never left the temple." Her life's work was to praise the Lord and to pray for the people. She would pray for her family and friends, for the leaders of her nation, for the spiritual life of her people, for those who ruled the land, for God's kingdom to come, and for His will to be done on earth as it is in heaven.

The name Anna means "God is gracious." Some people may have challenged her and said that her name was actually an oxymoron based on the events of her life. God is gracious? He took away your husband when you were just a young bride. Do you really believe God is gracious? But Anna is a Hidden Hero with a divine perspective of her life. She would remind all of us that the death of her husband was simply an opportunity to celebrate her union to the Lord. She would be quick to rebuke those who referred to her as a widow. "Do you think I have been a widow these past eighty-four years? Oh no! I have been married to the One who has called me His Bride," she might have said.

Anna's vocation was to praise and to pray. God has few saints like her on earth. He has plenty of people who are willing to preach. He has quite a few who do not shy away from the spotlight. Many, many gladly take the place of honor. But

He has few people who are willing to praise with all their being, and even fewer who feel called to make prayer and fasting the controlling ministry of their lives. Anna's vocation was simple: She was called to praise, and she was called to pray. The work she did, she completed unto the Lord—and He was certainly well pleased.

The Vision of the Saint

How rewarding that work must have seemed when Anna took that child in her hands: "Coming up to them at that very moment, she gave thanks to God and spoke about the child to all who were looking forward to the redemption of Jerusalem" (Luke 2:38). It was truly the greatest day in Anna's life, the day her lifelong prayers were answered.

The day began like any other day. Anna probably woke up that morning at the usual time. With her poor old bones and joints all stiff, she took a little while to get going. She dressed, went outside, picked up her pitcher, and made her way down to the well for water. There she would visit with other women from the neighborhood. Then she went back home to make herself a meager breakfast. She would then walk to her spot in the temple. Everyone knew it was her spot. Like many church members who have their own "pew," there is little doubt that Anna had her spot in the temple. Once secure in her rightful place she would begin to do what Anna does best. She would praise and pray.

But this day was different from any other day. Anna noticed a man and a woman coming. They were obviously poor and had with them a baby wrapped in a blanket. Then Anna saw an old man approach them. She knew the old man. Simeon had a reputation. He was devout in so many ways, but he kept talking—some would say foolishness—about how he had this vision about the Messiah. Anna couldn't help overhearing what Simeon said as he intercepted the couple and took the baby in his arms:

"Sovereign Lord, as you have promised,
   you now dismiss your servant in peace.
For my eyes have seen your salvation,
   which you have prepared in the sight of all people,
a light for revelation to the Gentiles
   and for glory to your people Israel." (Luke 2:29–32)

Anna's heart must have leaped inside her. Although she was well past the century mark in age, she must have felt like a young school girl whose pounding heart was made alive by the presence of the boy she longed to see. It was the Lord! Hallelujah! He'd come! Of course! Of course! He was to come as a baby. A virgin was to conceive and bear a Son. And so our Hidden Hero did was she does best—Anna burst into thanksgiving and praise.

She now had a new vocation. She began to make known the arrival of the Messiah to all who looked for redemption in Jerusalem. She knew every believer in town, and she couldn't wait to proclaim this news in a manner something like this: "He's here! He's alive! I've seen Him with my own eyes, I've held Him in my arms, and His name is Jesus. Keep your eyes and hearts open. Be sure you are ready."

Ready indeed. She had been ready every day for eighty-four years, and now her hope was realized. How she and Simeon must have laughed together after Jesus and His parents were on their way. And how they must have been saddened by those who weren't ready, even though everything they had longed for was being fulfilled right before their eyes. How many are like that today, sitting in church week after week, waiting for the Messiah but completely unaware of the times He seeks to woo them with His presence? How many are seeking after Him, reminding Him of His promises and imploring Him patiently yet impatiently to come quickly? Anna stands in the Hall of Hidden Heroes, speaking to us all: "Seek Him. Long for Him. Search Him. Be ready to be surprised by Him. Wait for Him as one whose very life depends on Him. Who knows?" She looks past you, beyond time, remembering that day so long ago as her voice fades into a wonderful memory, "Who knows?" she repeats. "When you least expect it…"

A Modern-Day Hidden Hero

She is so much like Anna. She *is* the Anna of the twenty-first century. She is known in our church as Gladys but in my eyes she is Anna. Like this great woman of faith, Gladys is called by God to pray and to praise. Each time I have a prayer request for which I know I need to call in the "big guns," I go first to Gladys and share my heart and request her intercession.

Gladys is well into her eighties today but is still a beautiful and vibrant woman of God. Each Sunday I see her arrive early for worship in order to prepare to assist in leading God's people in praise. Remember, I said that Gladys is not only like Anna in her faithfulness in prayer but also in her praise. I cannot even describe to you the inspiration she brings our church family and especially our worship team as she faithfully makes her way down the long aisles of the church, her cane in one hand and her violin in the other. She struggles to make it up the stairs and then gracefully takes her place among the other orchestra players and rehearses as she prepares for the music of praise that is to be shared in this day of worship. I can't tell you the times I have watched her playing in the orchestra and suddenly she is overwhelmed with a sense of the Spirit of God. She stops playing long enough to raise her bow hand to the Lord, welcoming Him with her praise.

Yes, Gladys is absolutely a modern day Hidden Hero and an *almost* perfect illustration of her New Testament counterpart. I said "almost" perfect replica of Anna only for the reason that Gladys is not a widow. She and Arthur, the 94-year-old love of her life, continue to faithfully serve the Lord

Jesus every single day. The two remain in love with one another and completely in love with the Savior they live to praise!

CHAPTER 12

Simon of Cyrene: Divine Interruption

◈

Then the governor's soldiers took Jesus into the Praetorium and gathered the whole company of soldiers around him. They stripped him and put a scarlet robe on him, and then twisted together a crown of thorns and set it on his head. They put a staff in his right hand and knelt in front of him and mocked him. "Hail, king of the Jews!" they said. They spit on him, and took the staff and struck him on the head again and again. After they had mocked him, they took off the robe and put his own clothes on him. Then they led him away to crucify him. As they were going out, they met a man from Cyrene, named Simon, and they forced him to carry the cross. (Matt. 27:27–32)

For Simon, who had traveled to Jerusalem from North Africa for a special purpose, it was nothing more than an irritation, an interruption in his day. He had traveled so far in hope that this day would be a celebration of his religion. But this interruption brought him face to face with a personal crisis and the humiliation of a convicted man's cross. This strong Jewish man from another country, most likely a black man according to later accounts from Acts, certainly would have resented the fact that soldiers would choose him for the tragic task. It would be hard not to see the blatant racism of the day, yet the Romans had swords and he'd have to do what they said.

Little did he realize that this was a divine interruption, an unexpected crisis for an eternal purpose. He would carry the cross, not from a willing heart but with resentment every step of this brief walk. He hated the Romans for singling him out and felt no pity for this condemned man who was so weakened by His scourging that He couldn't even carry his own cross. Yes, this was a divine interruption, one that would change Simon's life.

For those of us on this side of the cross, such a request would not bring such resentment. Instead, we would consider it an honor to serve our beloved Savior. Of course, you would do the same. Or would you? As we consider this chapter's Hidden Hero, we are confronted with a cross and a crisis awaiting every person who is stopped in his or her tracks with a divine interruption. For Simon, not only would his own life be changed. His family would be changed. His nation would be changed. His continent would be changed. Beyond that, he would provide a testimony that we continue to speak of today, two thousand years later.

Have you ever wondered how God will use divine interruptions in your life? Think of the times when you had everything all planned, and something went "wrong" that turned out to be just right. The pattern of Simon's divine interruption is not dissimilar to that which we experience even today: a new demand, a new direction, and a new devotion, all because of God's divine recasting of what we think we ought to be doing.

Consider the new demand placed upon Simon of Cyrene. The text, in Matthew 27:32, says the Roman soldiers "forced" him to carry the cross. The word "forced" is a word related to an ancient custom. The technique was used by both the Roman government and royal Persian couriers. These individuals had the authority, at any stage in their journey, to demand or commandeer anyone they deemed suitable to carry precious cargo or correspondence to a desired destination. This is the same principle Jesus spoke of when He said, "If someone forces you to go one mile, go with him two miles" (Matt. 5:41). When the Savior spoke these words about the demands of the Roman soldiers, He almost certainly was looking forward into the life of Simon and the divine interruption that would bring them face to face.

The very nature of the phrase "divine interruptions" indicates there is a message that God is communicating to you. The challenge of a divine interruption lies in the choices we make in responding to it. If we are not careful, we will view them only as one of life's everyday irritations, brush them aside, and move on with our life never stopping to consider the demand of the moment. So how can you tell the difference between a divine interruption and normal life interruption? Divine interruptions normally involve a crisis, and they always call for a commitment on your part.

On March 13, 2005, a young woman from Atlanta by the name of Ashley Smith was confronted with a divine interruption when an escaped convict and killer of four suddenly showed up at her apartment. This divine interruption forced Ashley to face the dilemma of reacting in fear or responding by faith.

"I believe God brought him to my door," Smith said of the man who was accused of shooting four people. "You're here in my apartment for some reason," she told him. Smith reported that she asked the killer if she could share with him something she had been reading. She then took a best-selling book, *The Purpose Driven Life*, and shared with the suspect how even his life meant something to God. She told him that his life did have purpose and discussed how God was using her life in the midst of this divine interruption. The captor released his hostage and turned himself in, renewed in the knowledge that even his tragic life could have a purpose if he paid attention to his own divine interruption.[25]

What do we know about today's Hidden Hero? We know there were colonies of Jews who lived outside Judea. Simon was from Cyrene, in northern Africa, which today would be Libya. He was on a pilgrimage to Jerusalem for the Passover. He had two sons, Alexander and Rufus, mentioned by the Gospel writer Mark and by Paul in the book of Romans.

The note in Microsoft Outlook from Simon's PDA would have been short and intentional: "Arrive at Jerusalem and participate in Passover." He just happened to be walking into the city as the crowd of Roman soldiers were walking out of the city, bringing Jesus. The itinerant preacher had just been beaten by order of the Roman governors and could barely stand, much less carry His own cross to the place of death. Simon would pause on the side of the road, allowing the authorities to pass but still standing oblivious to the significance of the events of this experience.

Simon's entire day was about to suddenly change...no, his entire *life* was about to change. Divine interruptions can bring new demands on an already difficult life. That's the very reason many people ignore these God-given opportunities. They rationalize in the midst of their divine interruption, "I can't do one more thing. I am so busy right now. I have my own life to live. I don't need this crisis right now." Many people dismiss divine interruptions because they can't comprehend how they can reconcile this new demand on their life with their own plans.

Divine interruptions are demanding by intention. Were they not often presented in the form of a crisis, then we would likely miss even more of these eternal opportunities. Simon's divine interruption was even more profound and had some distinctive but unsavory characteristics:

Shame: Listen to what the writer of Hebrews said about the cross: "Let us fix our eyes on Jesus, the author and perfecter of our faith, who for the joy set before him endured the cross, scorning its shame, and sat down at the right hand of the throne of God" (Heb. 12:2). The word shame in the Greek is a reference to "that which is covered," and it refers to our vulnerability should we be exposed. Simon, by his very presence near Jesus, is now exposed as he responds to the demand on his life to carry the cross. But once any individual takes up the cross, the days of secrecy are over. We have come out of darkness and have identified with Him in His light. The shame of our sin is exposed in the cross of Christ.

Suffering: As the weight of that wooden cross sank into Simon's shoulder, he obviously experienced physical suffering. What was physically true of Simon must also be spiritually true of us today. Read 1 Pet. 2:21: "To this you were called, because Christ suffered for you, leaving you an example, that you should follow in his steps." The word "suffered" in the Greek means "to bear the weight." Obviously, we cannot bear the weight for our sin. That is something that only Christ can do. But we can share in His sufferings when we understand that the demands of the cross insist we die to ourselves.

Sacrifice: The demand of the cross also includes sacrifice. For Christ, it was the sacrifice of His life for ours. For Simon, the demand this day would be the sacrifice of his time, his reputation, and his own plans in order to be identified with Christ. Paul reminds each of us of the demand of that sacrifice. Galatians 2:20 says this: "I have been crucified with Christ and I no longer live, but Christ lives in me. The life I live in the body, I live by faith in the Son of God, who loved me and gave himself for me."

When we see that by relying on Christ we'll survive the shame, suffering, and sacrifice of the new demand, we'll be able to walk more resolutely in a new direction. Mark, in his

Gospel account, adds something that Matthew doesn't include. Mark says this: "A certain man from Cyrene, Simon, the father of Alexander and Rufus, was passing by on his way in from the country, and they forced him to carry the cross" (Mark 15:21). Mark notes that Simon was "on his way in from the country." This illustrates the second principle about divine interruptions. They not only present you with new demands on your life, but they also insist on a new direction in your life. Simon would be forced to change directions by this divine interruption. He was headed into the city prior to being confronted with the divine interruption, and now he is walking in another direction.

This was more than just a simple change of directions; this was a spiritual turning point in Simon's life. No one can bear the cross of Christ without experiencing a revolutionary change.

Would Simon be one of those Jesus was referring to earlier in His ministry? In Luke 9:23, He said this: "If anyone would come after me, he must deny himself and take up his cross daily and follow me." When we are confronted with a divine interruption, our desires and designs will change so that we may follow Jesus Christ. Once the demand on your life has required you to pick up the cross, you will find yourself walking a new direction. Paul put it this way: "The old has gone, the new has come!" (2 Cor. 5:17). Simon was headed in one direction, was confronted with a divine interruption, and immediately began walking in a different direction. The change is the long-lasting evidence of the cross, the crisis, the divine interruption.

In the midst of this new direction, Simon was surprised with a new devotion. One truth we need to understand about divine interruptions is that while there are demands, there are also dividends awaiting the individual who is willing to walk by faith! With a new direction in following Christ comes a new devotion, which results in spiritual dividends.

When Sir Walter Raleigh spread his beautiful new cloak

over the mud so that Queen Elizabeth might walk without getting her shoes dirty, he was shrewd enough to know that nothing is lost when it is given to royalty. "He shall have his reward," was the queen's reply in response to the young man's gesture. She granted him an estate of twelve-thousand acres in Ireland. She also gave him trade privileges and the right to colonize in America. In 1585, she made him a knight. Indeed, in a very true sense, it is impossible to deny one's self for our King. His return is swift and vastly exceeds anything we've given.

When you consider the divine interruption of our Hidden Hero, you see the personal sacrifice that demanded a new direction, resulting in a life of new devotion. This new devotion in Simon's life was seen in two obvious areas:

New Devotion in His Faith: When Luke writes about the leaders who taught and ministered in the church at Antioch, he states, "In the church at Antioch there were prophets and teachers: Barnabas, Simeon called Niger, Lucius of Cyrene…" (Acts 13:1). Most biblical scholars maintain that this is the same Simon who carried the cross. Indeed, some suggest that he was a black man since he came from Libya in North Africa and was surnamed Niger. If this is correct then Simon became one of the greatest blessings in the life of the early church. Dr. Alan Cole writes: "Simon of Cyrene might be taken homiletically as a picture of every disciple, bearing the Lord's cross for Him. How we need men of the cross in the church of Jesus Christ today! Men who understand that Calvary is a reality where sin is judged, self crucified, and the Spirit outpoured."

I love what Dr. Stephen Olford writes in a commentary on Simon: "We can never compute the blessing which Simon has become to the world since that first Good Friday. Throughout the centuries the story of cross-bearing, at the moment of our Savior's greatest need, has converted and inspired millions. In this sense, Simon has been honored above Peter, James, John, or any other disciple who forsook the Master and fled, leaving

Him to carry His cross alone."

New Devotion in His Family: Again, Mark reminds us…"A certain man from Cyrene, Simon, the father of Alexander and Rufus, was passing by on his way in from the country, and they forced him to carry the cross." When you consider the great blessings of this divine interruption in Simon's life, you cannot ignore the spiritual blessing he found in his home. This man was so transformed by the power of Christ that the blessing he found in the crisis of the cross was passed on to those he loved in his own home. Mark refers to his two sons, Alexander and Rufus, as well-known believers in the early Christian church. Mark makes a reference to Rufus as one of the leaders of the Roman church, and Paul acknowledges the impact Simon had on his family in Rom. 16:13: "Greet Rufus, chosen in the Lord, and his mother, who has been a mother to me, too." What a home this must have been! Think of it…it all begin with a divine interruption in the middle of a man's day.

We would do well today to be sensitive to the divine interruptions in our life and to know that the only answer to the crisis that faces all of us in life is to follow the example of today's Hidden Hero as we too take up our cross and follow Christ. Only when the power of the cross penetrates our hearts will His power change our lives, change the relationship between husband and wife, change the lives of parents and children, change our churches, and eventually change our world in which we live. Today's divine interruptions come in different shapes. The key to victory is to stop long enough to realize your divine interruption is a gift from God. Yes, there will be demands, and those demands may result in shame, suffering, and sacrifice. But with the new demands you will also find new direction, which leads to devotion and a changed life that will benefit you, your family, your church, and the community in which you live.

A Modern-Day Hidden Hero

Common sense should tell you that Simon was a strong man, a man who would easily be identified in the crowd as a man of muscle. What you probably would not have been able to discern is the fact that Simon's physical strength was surpassed by his spiritual strength and influence.

My friend John is a pretty strong reflection of the Hidden Hero from this chapter. John is a good example not because he, like Simon, is a black man. Nor is John the best model simply because of his physical strength. (In this category, Simon couldn't hold a candle to John. After all, John won the world powerlifting championships not once but twice!) Actually, John best represents this chapter's Hidden Hero because he is a quiet giant who possesses some of the greatest spiritual wisdom and insight of anyone I have met.

Through the years, I have seen John come face to face with one divine interruption after another. In every situation this giant of the faith has had the courage and conviction to look beyond his own personal crisis and diligently seek to understand what the Father was trying to teach him. As the strength coach for the Miami Dolphins of the National Football League, John has to make the personal and professional transition in working with five different head coaches. Remember, there is about as much job security for an assistant coach in the NFL as there was for a gladiator facing the hungry lions. Yet in every transition, John has looked to prayerfully find the activity of God and then has quickly rested in the Father's leadership to walk him through the difficult waters of change.

Perhaps one of the reasons John has worked with five different head coaches is the fact that each leader who takes over the team recognizes that this Hidden Hero brings far more to the table than simply producing the finest physical specimen possible to put into battle on Sunday afternoons. They have seen the character, integrity, and calming influence John has in the locker room and the phenomenal rapport he has with each player. As I have visited with the players through the years, I have asked them privately why John is different. Without exception each one has told me it is because he cares.

Simon did not look forward to hefting the cross and carrying it for the Savior that day two thousand years ago, any more than John welcomed the news that his youngest son and wife had been in a terrible car accident. His son's life was in the balance as paramedics rushed him to the emergency room. At the hospital, I stood once again beside this mountain of a man and watched him lay that giant hand on his little boy's head. He turned to me and said, "Pastor, pray with me for God's will to be done. This cross is heavy, and I need some help carrying it." John, you didn't need my help but God allowed me to be with you at that moment to again witness the amazing godly character that comes from a man of spiritual strength who has learned the value of taking up his cross daily and following the Master. I'm thankful today that you and your son walk together in the grace of God's saving power, willing to do whatever the Master asks of you.

CHAPTER 13

CSI Jerusalem: Mystery Solved

Considered perhaps the greatest of all the Renaissance artists, Michelangelo was not one to keep his opinion to himself. Contemplating the depiction of Jesus by his fellow artists, he reportedly pounced upon them: "Why do you keep filling gallery after gallery with endless pictures on the one theme of Christ in weakness, Christ on the cross, and most of all, Christ hanging dead? Why do you concentrate on the passing episode as if it were the last work, as if the curtain dropped on Him with disaster and defeat? That dreadful scene lasted only a few hours. But to the unending eternity Christ is alive; the stone has been rolled away and He rules and reigns and triumphs!"

Michelangelo's colleagues were living in the dark shadow of Good Friday. But the great artist, who had known so much loss and personal pain, knew his only hope was the promise of the wonderful Sunday we call Easter. One of Michelangelo's amazing but lesser known masterpieces is a sculpture called *The Risen Christ*. Christ stands strong, as conqueror of the cross, with knowing eyes and a forceful presence in marble. Many scholars contend that the reason this work is so compelling is that it is one of the works Michelangelo did not quite finish. It was if the artist was saying, "The work of our risen Christ continues. It did not end on the cross and it did not end with the resurrection. He stands risen to reign! The work of the cross is finished, but the work of our Savior continues throughout eternity."

Of course, such a perspective is easier when you're sculpting fifteen hundred years after the events of that original Easter week. But for those first followers of Jesus, Easter Sunday started without any reason for celebration. The first Easter morning did not seem like a great triumph. In fact it seemed like a great injustice or misfortune because it appeared a crime had been committed; the body of Jesus was gone, and the tomb was empty! We would need some expert help to solve this mystery of the ultimate Hidden Hero. Let's take a few moments to examine the scene of that first Easter morning, from the eyewitness report in John 20:1–9:

> Early on the first day of the week, while it was still dark, Mary Magdalene went to the tomb and saw that the stone had been removed from the entrance. So she came running to Simon Peter and the other disciple, the one Jesus loved, and said, 'They have taken the Lord out of the tomb, and we don't know where they have put him!' So Peter and the other disciple started for the tomb. Both were running, but the other disciple outran Peter and reached the tomb first. He bent over and looked in at the strips of linen lying there but did not go in. Then Simon Peter, who was behind him, arrived and went into the tomb. He saw the strips of linen lying there, as well as the burial cloth that had been around Jesus' head. The cloth was folded up by itself, separate from the linen. Finally the other disciple, who had reached the tomb first, also went inside. He saw and believed. (They still did not understand from Scripture that Jesus had to rise from the dead.)

Solving the mystery of the ultimate Hidden Hero is not easy. In looking at the crime scene team from Jerusalem, we can learn some key principles for our life in our search for Jesus Christ and our daily walk with Him. The CSI team that day involved three experts: a woman of uncertain background named Mary Magdalene, a former fisherman named Peter, and a young man named John. Each of the three came to a different conclusion.

Mary: "It was a tragedy!"
Consider this account: "Early on the first day of the week, while it was still dark, Mary Magdalene went to the tomb and saw that the stone had been removed from the entrance. So she came running to Simon Peter and the other disciple, the one Jesus loved, and said, 'They have taken the Lord out of the tomb, and we don't know where they have put him!'"

We might call this first CSI Jerusalem scene "The Mystery of the Open Tomb." Mary saw the stone removed. This was just before dawn while it was still dark. This would have been the easiest time of day to travel out to the area of the tomb. Mary finds the tomb open. What a shock this must have been.

What was the reason for the sealed tomb? The tomb had a strong seal on purpose, so the government could ensure that no one tampered with the evidence. The tomb had a large groove along the base with a large circular stone to close the entrance. The stone was rolled into place by several strong soldiers and became nearly impossible to remove. The tomb was then officially sealed. The stone was then sealed by either clay or wax to make it air tight. The tomb of Jesus was also given the signet seal of the emperor, making it a capital crime to tamper with the tomb. Just to be sure, Pilate stationed Roman soldiers to guard the tomb. He wanted to be sure that nothing—divine or otherwise—interfered with his sentence.

What, then, was the reaction to the open tomb? When Mary sees that the body of Jesus is gone her first instinct is to run and get Peter to tell him what had happened. Was Mary going to share good news with the others? No! Mary had believed that the body of Jesus had been stolen: "They have taken the Lord out of the tomb, and we don't know where they have put him!" From Mary's point of view, this was a crisis on top of the tragedy. It never occurred to her that Jesus had been raised from the dead. This is the reaction the majority of the people in the world have to Jesus Christ. He was a good man who met a tragic death. That was Mary's deduction from her investigation of the facts, but it was wrong.

Mary was focused on the tragedy. Here were the facts as she knew them. First, Jesus was dead. This was a severe setback to the disciples because they never understood the fact that Jesus was going to die. So, when Jesus was crucified, they could not deal with the situation. Second, Jesus' body was missing and presumed stolen. The body of Jesus was simply gone from the tomb, and the only logical explanation was that the body was stolen. Third, no one knew where the body was located and what had been done to the body. This was a great crisis of faith for Mary, and her reaction was to panic. How do you see this Jesus of the Easter story? What kind of tragedies are in your life? The tragedy of a loved one who has passed away. The tragedy of lost relationships, maybe divorce, separation, or strained family relations. The tragedy of lost opportunities, like time with family, influence on a friend, impact in your community. Financial tragedy, like a lost job, a missed promotion, a failed business. The first of our CSI Jerusalem investigators looked at the scene, and her response was to focus on the tragedy and leave the situation in the realm of the physical. Her only explanation was found in what people can do, not what God might do.

Peter: "All I saw was a tomb."

Now consider Peter's account: "So Peter and the other disciple started for the tomb. Both were running, but the other disciple outran Peter and reached the tomb first. He bent over and looked in at the strips of linen lying there but did not go in. Then Simon Peter, who was behind him, arrived and went into the tomb. He saw the strips of linen lying there, as well as the burial cloth that had been around Jesus' head. The cloth was folded up by itself, separate from the linen."

Peter, never one not to jump to a quick conclusion, responds to Mary's report by running to the crime scene. Unfortunately, he's so focused on the facts that he forgets his faith. Peter's investigative partner, John, arrives at the tomb first. But while he's still assessing the situation, Peter runs right past him and takes the first steps into the tomb. He begins a thorough investigation and wastes no time in his attempt to solve the mystery. These are the facts. No body: Jesus was definitely gone. No theft: The burial linens were still in place so it's not likely that someone would steal the body but leave the linens. No disturbance: The burial cloth was folded upon itself. It had been used to cover the head of Jesus, but now it was doubled up as if what had been under it just mysteriously disappeared without shifting the cloth in any manner. This would have been impossible, unless there was a miraculous removal of the body. This is one of the most striking evidences for the resurrection. There was no indication of struggle to remove the body; if someone stole the body he would have certainly either taken the shroud or not spent the time folding it and putting it back into place.

These facts should have given Peter all the evidence he needed to draw on his faith. Instead, he stood dumbfounded in his deduction. The evidence that Peter saw was indeed conclusive. The body of Jesus was gone from the tomb. Peter did not process the information. Peter did not understand the scope of what had happened. He focused on merely answering the question, "What happened here?" He couldn't come to a conclusion and instead stood clueless. Mary's response was emotional. Peter's response was emotional and intellectual.

Neither could get past their uncertainties to uncover the real story.

John: "This is a triumph!"

Let's look at the same account, the same words, but with the rest of the story intact: "So Peter and the other disciple started for the tomb. Both were running, but the other disciple outran Peter and reached the tomb first. He bent over and looked in at the strips of linen lying there but did not go in. Then Simon Peter, who was behind him, arrived and went into the tomb. He saw the strips of linen lying there, as well as the burial cloth that had been around Jesus' head. The cloth was folded up by itself, separate from the linen. *Finally the other disciple, who had reached the tomb first, also went inside. He saw and believed.*"

John investigates the tomb and combines the emotional response of seeing the empty tomb with the intellectual response of seeing the facts. But he takes it one step further, applying the spiritual response of faith that allows him to see this day as a triumph and not a tragedy. John sees the exact same things that both Mary and Peter saw. John did not miss anything that Peter saw in the tomb, and Peter saw all of things that John saw that day. However, there was a great difference. As a matter of fact, it is an eternal difference in their personal reaction. John saw the linens, the burial cloth and the most obvious evidence of all: the empty tomb.

John got to the tomb first because he outran Peter. John looked in but did not enter without Peter. Why didn't John just go right in when he arrived? It seems strange that John would not immediately run into the tomb after looking in and seeing that the body of Jesus was gone. I believe John was attempting to process the event and, by faith, was applying what Jesus had taught them. The facts were not merely enough for John. There is a vast difference between knowing and believing. John applied the facts to his faith and moved from head knowledge to heart knowledge: "Finally the other disciple, who had reached the tomb first, also went inside. He saw and believed." John saw the triumph of the empty tomb. The body of Jesus was gone and gone in a miraculous way. John believed that Jesus did exactly what He said He would do to defeat death. John saw and believed that the Father had raised Jesus from the dead.

Maybe you are like Mary. You have placed your focus on the tragedies that have burdened you. Perhaps you are like Peter. You know the facts of the resurrection but never applied that faith and knowledge to your heart. Do you have emotional religion? Intellectual religion? Or do you have a relationship with Jesus Christ that involves your emotion, your intellect, and your faith—a faith that enables you to live in triumph as you remember the empty tomb? It is time today to move from the facts to faith.

CHAPTER 14

Déjà You: Joy Restored

※

Now that same day two of them were going to a village called Emmaus, about seven miles from Jerusalem. They were talking with each other about everything that had happened. As they talked and discussed these things with each other, Jesus himself came up and walked along with them; but they were kept from recognizing him.

He asked them, "What are you discussing together as you walk along?"

They stood still, their faces downcast. One of them, named Cleopas, asked him, "Are you only a visitor to Jerusalem and do not know the things that have happened there in these days?"

"What things?" he asked.

"About Jesus of Nazareth," they replied. "He was a prophet, powerful in word and deed before God and all the people. The chief priests and our rulers handed him over to be sentenced to death, and they crucified him; but we had hoped that he was the one who was going to redeem Israel. And what is more, it is the third day since all this took place. In addition, some of our women amazed us. They went to the tomb early this morning but didn't find his body. They came and told us that they had seen a vision of angels, who said he was alive. Then some of our companions went to the tomb and found it just as the women had said, but him they did not see."

He said to them, "How foolish you are, and how slow of heart to believe all that the prophets have spoken! Did not the Christ have to suffer these things and then enter his glory?" And beginning with Moses and all the Prophets, he explained to them what was said in all the Scriptures concerning himself.

As they approached the village to which they were going, Jesus acted as if he were going farther. But they urged him strongly, "Stay with us, for it is nearly evening; the day is almost over." So he went in to stay with them.

When he was at the table with them, he took bread, gave thanks, broke it and began to give it to them. Then their eyes were opened and they recognized him, and he disappeared from their sight. They asked each other, "Were not our hearts burning within us while he talked with us on the road and opened the Scriptures to us?"

They got up and returned at once to Jerusalem. There they found the Eleven and those with them, assembled together and saying, "It is true! The Lord has risen and has appeared to Simon." Then the two told what had happened on the way, and how Jesus was recognized by them when he broke the bread. (Luke 24:13–35)

Just when life couldn't seem any worse...these were just two of the many who had put their hope—all their hope, for today and for the eternity to come—in the carpenter from Nazareth who turned out to be so much more. This story reminds us how easy it is for the unexpected certainties in life to rob of us of our joy, even as believers. We must expect that our Hidden Hero must have been thinking "déjà vu" as he walked sadly away from what he thought was the death of his dreams.

Cleopas teaches us that every one of us will experience the unexpected disappointments in life. And, unexpectedly even for him, Cleopas also becomes a model of how Jesus can take even our greatest tragedies and turn them into triumphs to restore our lost joy. Cleopas was not one of the "official" apostles but certainly was a disciple of Christ. He and his companion had turned their backs on the scene of their greatest pain, the death of Jesus. With its tragedy of the cross and the death of all they had hoped for seared in their minds, they did what many of us try to do when the pain is this fresh…they walked away!

Their walk would take them to Emmaus, some seven miles away. Little did Cleopas know that this journey had a purpose; Jesus would meet him at the depth of his despair and begin the process of simply reminding him of the truths he already knew. By the end of the journey, Cleopas will not only find joy, he will also encounter Jesus and establish a memory marker he will never forget. Déjà vu? No, for Cleopas it will be "Déjà you!" Our Hidden Hero will help us identify three important facts we must remember when tragedy has robbed us of the victory we have in Christ.

A Blinding Presence

Consider again Cleopas and his friend. They're walking along, not wanting to relive the pain they've just experienced. Then the One they're talking about walks up. Sometimes our broken hearts give us bad hearing. One of the most important principles about our walk of faith with Jesus is that He will always draw near to those who find the pain so overwhelming.

Yet those painful times also seem to be the times we're least likely to look for His presence. Even in the midst of absolute pain—times when we shouldn't be looking to anyone else except the Healer—we are blinded to His presence by our own hurt and brokenness. Cleopas met our Hidden Hero this first Easter morning, and He has joined men and women ever since as they have walked that lonely road of pain, disappointment, and devastation. The fact that we must see is that even in our deepest and darkest valley, even the valley of the shadow of death, we have no need to fear, for He is with us.

Each of us will walk down this path. Many have walked this path before, and some are walking this path today. It is the path of pain, and like the disciples we may feel as if our faith has failed, dreams have been dashed, love has been lost. Cleopas was devastated because in his heart the faith that he thought was so certain had failed. This is evidenced by what he says to Jesus in verse 18: "Are you only a visitor to Jerusalem and do not know the things that have happened there in these days?" Cleopas believed when Christ rode into Jerusalem on that Palm Sunday He was the Promised One who would redeem Israel. He believed Jesus would drive out the Romans and establish the messianic kingdom. But our Hidden Hero watched Jesus die and watched as they took His body off the cross and buried Him in the tomb. When Jesus died, so did the faith of Cleopas.

Obviously in our world today there are people whose faith has been shaken. Many have found their religion has failed. They've seen tragedy in the world: world wars and wars in the home, famine and despair and hunger and homelessness, merciless tyrants and good leaders who didn't live up to their billing, unfulfilled expectations and unexpected disruptions. The sad result is a faith that is shaken. More than just his faith, Cleopas also had the hope of his life shattered. He had enough religious knowledge to know the meaning of all the talk that spoke about a victory on the third day. Cleopas heard Jesus say that in three days the temple of His body would be raised up, but three days had gone by and nothing had happened.

His faith was shaken, his hope was shattered, but what is even more tragic was the fact that his love was lost. Cleopas loved this man whom they called the Messiah. He had seen Him perform miracles. He had seen Him touch the heads of little children. He had watched Him break bread and multiply fish to feed the multitudes. He had seen Him raise the dead and heal the leper…all of this with his own eyes. But now He was gone, and with His death, a love was lost.

Nothing is more painful than love that is lost! Love lost through death or divorce is still love lost. In the heart of our Hidden Hero Jesus is gone, He's buried, and He's lost. How very tragic that our pain blinds us to His presence! If only we would open our eyes, we would see the Lord walking with us, talking to us, and drawing near to us in our pain. His peace could replace our pain, but we stubbornly hold on to the heartache and fail to see the truth of Jesus drawing near to us, sent by the Father in heaven to join us on this painful path, ready to discuss our failed faith, our dreams that have been destroyed, and the most painful of all, our love that has been lost.

There's something amazing about the encounter of Jesus with our Hidden Hero. He patiently waited for His followers to recognize Him. He continued to speak. He never withdrew, never turned His back, and never walked away in frustration. He continued to walk with the pain-filled disciple, lovingly challenging the thinking, the thought process, the faith of those who follow Him. He is the one who started the conversation. Our healing always is initiated by Jesus Christ. Jesus never meets anyone along the painful path of life without loving them enough to start a conversation. Because of His love and compassion, He has meet us where we are in order to expose the unbelief the pain has caused. He has also come to meet us, to love us, and to renew us with His life.

Transforming Truth

There comes a point in our walk down the path of pain where we find Jesus not only loving us enough to walk and talk with us but also loving us enough to confront us when we fail to see the truth. He came to us in order that He might expose the emptiness and unbelief where pain has replaced His promises. Jesus confronts us with truth, a truth that will transform our lives. Pay close attention to the manner in which Jesus shares this transforming truth and the progression in the life of our Hidden Hero.

Truth Revisited: "He said to them, 'How foolish you are, and how slow of heart to believe all that the prophets have spoken! Did not the Christ have to suffer these things and then enter his glory?' And beginning with Moses and all the Prophets, he explained to them what was said in all the Scriptures concerning himself." Beginning with Moses, Jesus began to revisit the truth that our Hidden Hero had learned his entire life. In revisiting the truth, He was reminding Cleopas that He was the fulfillment of God's law. In the truth Jesus revisited, He showed that He was the fulfillment of God's life. In the truth revisited, Jesus revealed He was the fulfillment of God's love. The concrete truth is evidenced when Jesus reminds our Hidden Hero that He was the fulfillment of all the Scriptures.

Truth Revealed: "Did not the Christ have to suffer these things and then enter his glory?" Now Jesus begins to address the very event of which they were speaking when He found them on the road. In this truth, He is revealing that He was the historic fulfillment of what He said would happen. Prophecy had now become history. The problem Cleopas had was his difficulty in accepting what had already been revealed in Bible prophecy.

In his book *The Gospel According to St. Luke*, Dr. Leon Morris points out: "The prophets had spoken plainly enough, but the mind of Cleopas had not been quick enough to grasp what was meant. The word 'all' is important. Cleopas no doubt seized on the prediction of the glory of the Messiah, but it was quite another thing to take to heart the prophecies that pointed to the darker side of His mission…the passion was not simply a possibility that might or might not become actual, depending on the circumstances: it was necessary!"[26]

Truth Received: "They asked each other, 'Were not our hearts burning within us while he talked with us on the road and opened the Scriptures to us?' " As Jesus spoke with Cleopas, the disciple's heart began to burn within him. If you are prepared to recognize and receive the presence of the Lord Jesus on your journey in life, you will discover that conversation quickly turns to confrontation, which leads to conviction and ultimately will lead to commitment. Cleopas showed that no one can encounter the Lord Jesus and ever be the same again. He alone can change the tearful heart into a triumphant heart.

In more than thirty years in ministry, I've learned that one of the great indicators of truth that is transforming the life of a Christian is evidenced in their personal desire to spend time with Jesus. The reason many of us continue to have the spiritual hero hiding in our lives is that we would rather do anything than spend time alone with the Lover of our soul. The Savior never insists that you spend time with Him, and He will not barge in on your life without an invitation. You must revisit the truth and allow the truth to be revealed in your heart before you receive the truth that will ultimately transform your life. It all begins in His presence.

Déjà Vu Again

In order for Jesus to be made known in our lives, many times that requires some déjà vu. We must be willing to "remember!" To review the spiritual memory markers in our life and reflect on the power and the love of Christ as we recall how sufficient He was to meet our need. In the midst of our travels down the path of pain, we would do well to pause, reflect on His promise to us, and remember His love for us and how faithful He has been to us in our past.

As you ponder this truth the Spirit will reveal the truth that Jesus is continuing to walk by your side and is once again ready to take your path of pain and turn it into a place of praise in the midst of His presence. It is difficult when pain fills your heart. You may even know that Jesus is standing outside and knocking and calling to you to open your heart to His presence, but pity and pain are deadbolts that keep His promise and His presence out of your life. That all begins to change when you are willing to simply recognize who is standing right beside you and to know His desire to once again give you His love, His peace, His presence, His provision, and His protection, and to fill your heart with His praise. Some call it "déjà vu," but in our relationship with Christ it is always "deja you!"

A Modern-Day Hidden Hero

For John and Donna it was certainly a case of "déjà vu!" After all, they had dated for what seemed to be forever, and then after a short breakup and being apart for three months they found themselves back in each other's arms. However, this time the reconciliation was conditional. Donna realized that they both lived in a fast-paced world, and if they were to make it as a couple there needed to be some changes. (I do not use the words "fast-paced" lightly, as John is the seven-time world champion in super powerboat racing. Sports magazines refer to him as the "Michael Jordan" of powerboat racing.)

"We need to go to church. We need to have a spiritual foundation in our life if we are serious about getting married," Donna had insisted. John agreed, and their first visit to church came on a glorious Easter Sunday. As this glamorous couple sat in church, the Spirit of God opened their eyes to the truth of Scripture, and they both found themselves broken at the altar, giving their lives to Jesus Christ and recognizing Him as their personal Savior.

With this newfound faith came the desire to honor the sanctity of marriage, and they immediately begin to make plans. In the course of normal routine physical check-ups, Donna confronted John with the most devastating news he had ever received: "John, I have AIDS."

Hope hindered, faith fleeting, love lost? Blinded by the worst of circumstances, even after a remarkable experience with Jesus Himself? Understanding that pain blinds you to His promises...John and Donna definitely walked down the same devastating Emmaus road experience. Every person John received counsel from advised him against marrying Donna. From a worldly perspective, this really could be suicide. Yet the amazing realization of the new life both of these young adults had experienced in Christ provided them with the strength they needed to go forward in marriage.

The years have passed. John continues to add to his impressive career as "world's greatest powerboat racer." In the midst of the success, John and Donna continue to point people to the power of Christ and the change that results when you realize that Jesus is walking with you every minute of every day. Do they compare to Cleopas, the Hidden Hero of two thousand years ago, in how they handled the pain of their crisis? Déjà vu!

Conclusion

Thank you for sharing this journey with me in the discovery of the most neglected people in scripture… the Hidden Heroes. It has been my sincere prayer that as you walked through the lives of these individuals you were struck with one thought: "If God can do that through their lives…then why not mine?" Yes! That is exactly what I want you to see. There is a hidden hero in each of us, and God wants to transform that ordinary life into an extraordinary adventure.

As you've read this book, maybe you caught yourself thinking about your own friends and family members who would qualify for the title of Hidden Hero. I encourage you to identify them, and then take a moment and write them a letter and share with them how their life has impacted yours. Hidden Heroes never act for personal recognition. They act because it is the right thing to do, and because of obedience their lives are transformed. While they would never consider themselves heroes, it would still be a tremendous encouragement to affirm their faithfulness and to share with them how their words or actions have made a difference in your life. It is no secret that in the same book that provides us the Heroes of the Faith we are also given this instruction, "Let us encourage one another—and all the more as you see the Day approaching" (Heb. 10:25).

Throughout this book, I have shared a postscript for each Hidden Hero. I have given you real-life illustrations of the people who quietly and without fanfare made themselves available to the Lord. I wanted you to see the truth that Hidden Heroes are all around us. In fact, I will not be surprised if when I get to heaven I find out that it was the Hidden Heroes of this world who actually had the greatest impact.

I have saved my last modern-day example of a Hidden Hero for this final word. I have done this by intention. Many years ago, when I entered adulthood, God brought into my life the greatest Christian I have ever met. This woman is the most consistent and godly witness I have ever met. Is she perfect? No. She would be the first to tell you what she considers her imperfections. She would laugh if you attempted to refer to her as any kind of hero.

But I know her better than anyone does. I see the consistency of her spiritual walk. I see the daily time she spends in communion with Christ. I see her wisdom when faced with difficult challenges. I see her absolute love for the church. Most of all, I am the blessed recipient of her love. We have shared a partnership in love and marriage for more than three decades. We have grown up together, and yet she stills maintains that playful spirit of a young girl just in love. She is the model wife, and she is a model mom. The daughters God entrusted to our care have become a reflection of their mother's love, conviction, wisdom, and purity. Taylor and Jennifer and now my "son-in-love" Mason will all join with me in sharing the joy this Hidden Hero brings to our lives.

Years ago, in one of the most difficult times we have had together in ministry, Cynthia and I took a couple of days off to refocus and renew the call God has given to us in marriage and ministry. We were in a hotel in Dallas, and Cynthia was not feeling well. I slipped out early in the morning to get her some coffee and donuts. While I was driving, a song came on the radio. As I listened to the words, I was overwhelmed; every word in the song reflected my heart, my thoughts, and my love for my wife.

I drove for over an hour until I found a music store so I could purchase the song. Finally, I returned to the hotel and asked Cynthia to get dressed and come downstairs to the listen to something I heard on the radio. "It is really important to me that you hear this," I said. As we made our way to the parking lot and into the car, a light rain was now making its own beat on the windshield. In the midst of that overcast day I said, "I know that ministry at times is very difficult, and I know you have been wounded, but what you need to know is this: I need you, I love you, and I could never see myself living without you or serving without you. Please listen to these words, because they are the words of my heart to you." As I played the song, this is what she heard:

> It must have been cold there in my shadow,
> To never have sunlight on your face.
> You were content to let me shine, that's your way.
> You always walked a step behind.
>
> So I was the one with all the glory,
> While you were the one with all the strain.
> A beautiful face without a name for so long.
> A beautiful smile to hide the pain.
>
> Did you ever know that you're my hero,
> And everything I would like to be?
> I can fly higher than an eagle,
> For you are the wind beneath my wings.
>
> It might have appeared to go unnoticed,
> But I've got it all here in my heart.
> I want you to know I know the truth, of course I know it.
> I would be nothing without you.

Did you ever know that you're my hero?
You're everything I wish I could be.
I could fly higher than an eagle,
For you are the wind beneath my wings.

Did I ever tell you you're my hero?
You're everything, everything I wish I could be.
Oh, and I, I could fly higher than an eagle,
For you are the wind beneath my wings,
'cause you are the wind beneath my wings.

Oh, the wind beneath my wings.
You, you, you, you are the wind beneath my wings.
Fly, fly, fly away. you let me fly so high.
Oh, you, you, you, the wind beneath my wings.
Oh, you, you, you, the wind beneath my wings.

Fly, fly, fly high against the sky,
So high I almost touch the sky.
Thank you, thank you,
Thank God for you, the wind beneath my wings.[27]

Today, after more than thirty years together as partners, lovers, and best friends....Cynthia, you are still the wind beneath my wings. You will always and forever be my Hidden Hero. Thank you for allowing God to transform an ordinary life into what continues to be an extraordinary adventure! Love, Larry

About the Author

Dr. Larry L. Thompson has been senior pastor at the 12,000-member First Baptist Church of Fort Lauderdale since August 1994. He had previously served as pastor at Dauphin Way Baptist Church in Mobile, First Baptist Church in Merritt Island, First Baptist Church in Chickasha, First Liberty Baptist Church in Tulsa, and First Baptist Church in Hobart, Oklahoma. Pastor Thompson and his wife, Cynthia, have two daughters: Taylor (who attended Columbia University and Wheaton College) and Jennifer (who received her master's degree from Regent University).

Thompson's innovative methods feature a team approach to ministry which leads members in discovering their personal gifts, talents and passions to increase their effectiveness in helping others. With a background in theater and drama, he is known as a dynamic, personable, practical communicator. With a strong sense of the important experience of worship, Thompson's churches have been at forefront of evangelical praise, recording two pacesetting projects from Integrity Music (*God With Us* and *Let Your Glory Fall*, both with Don Moen) and the choral collection, *Whatever You Need, God Is*. *God With Us* received the Dove Award as "musical of the year" in 1994. He co-authored a Christmas drama called *Dickens' Christmas Journey*. More than three dozen churches have performed the original script.

Thompson's current church is host to the Fort Lauderdale Christmas Pageant, a million-dollar nationally televised holiday production. More than 50,000 South Florida residents make one of the Pageant's nineteen performances part of their Christmas season.

As author of the Watchman Prayer Ministry, Thompson has been featured on the Focus on the Family radio broadcast. The Watchman Prayer Ministry is an intercessory prayer program being used in more than 2,000 churches, a national prayer strategy which connects thousands of Christians in round-the-clock prayer. Thompson also developed the POP Strategy for evangelistic outreach and wrote the accompanying booklet, "The Path."

He received an honorary doctorate of letters from the University of Mobile for his efforts on behalf of international education and another from the California Graduate School of Theology for his work in church growth. He also received a Master of Arts in Ministry from Luther Rice Seminary. Thompson has served on the Board of Trustees at the University of Mobile, Oklahoma Baptist University and Cornerstone University. He was chairman of the board for the Little Lighthouse, a nonprofit school for the physically limited recognized by President George Bush with a "Thousand Points of Light" commendation.

Endnotes

[1] DeShazo, Lynn B. Ancient Words (Mobile, AL: Integrity's Hosanna Music)

[2] Kerry Keane. "The Lady Tennant Stradivari, A sublime violin with a fascinating provenance." [Online] cited 25 April 2005, available from <http://www.christies.com/home_page/object_week/object_week.asp>

[3] William Henry Hill, Arthur Frederick Hill, and Alfred Ebsworth Hill. *Antonio Stradivari: His Life and Work, 1644–1737.* 1902. Reprint. (New York: Dover, 1963)

[4] Martin Gayford. "The finest of all fiddlemakers." Arts.Telegraph, May 9, 2004. [online] cited 25 April 2005, available from <http://www.arts.telegraph.co.uk/arts/main.jhtml?xml=/arts/2004/09/05/bofab05.xml&sSheet=/arts/2004/09/05/botop.html>

[5] Cited by National Public Radio

[6] Charles Choi. "Secrets of the Stradivarius: An Interview with Joseph Nagyvary." ScientificAmerican.com. June 10, 2002. [online] cited 25 April 2005, available from <http://www.sciam.com/article.cfm? articleID=000BD557-2293-1CFD-93F6809EC5880000>

[7] Victor Harold Matthews, Mark W. Chavalas, and John H. Walton. *The IVP Bible Background Commentary: Old Testament*, electronic ed. (Downers Grove, IL: InterVarsity Press, 2000).

[8] 1 Chron. 23:1–5

[9] Percy A. Scholes, *The Oxford Companion to Music*, 10th ed. (New York: Oxford University Press, 1970), 454. Cited by Edith Schaeffer in *Forever Music* (Nashville: Thomas Nelson, 1986), 122

[10] Bach's Bible, known as the Calov Bible, is now in the collection at the Concordia Theological Seminary in St. Louis, Missouri

[11] Smith, Timothy A. Essay on "Fugue No. 20, A minor, Well-Tempered Clavier Book I."

[12] David W. Music, "Instruments in Church: A Collection of Source Documents." Studies in Liturgical Musicology, No. 7 (Lanham and London: Scarecrow Press, 1998).

[13] http://www.ccel.org/c/calvin/comment3/comm_vol08/htm/xxxix.htm (Calvin seemed to think instruments were acceptable for private devotion, just not assembled worship.)

[14] http://www.bible.ca/ef/topical-historical-quotes-about-music-in-worship.htm

[15] http://www.csmonitor.com/2004/0520/p01s01-ussc.html

[16] http://wikisource.org/wiki/The_Legend_of_Jubal (public domain)

[17] Eugene Peterson, *The Message*. (Colorado Springs: NavPress, 2002).

[18] http://www.drhorsehair.com/history.html

[19] Carl Frederich Keil and Franz Delitzsch. *Commentary on the Old Testament*. (Peabody, MA: Hendrickson, 2002)

[20] George Angus Fulton Knight. *Psalms: Volume 2*. The Daily Study Bible series. (Louisville: Westminster John Knox Press, 2001, c1982)

[21] You can read about Bill's personal story at http://www.thegoal.com/players/owners/rose_bill/rose_bill.html

[22] Steckoll, Solomon. The Temple Mount: An Illustrated History of Mount Moriah in Jerusalem (London: Tom Stacey Publishers, 1972)

[23] Thoreau, Henry David. *Walden; Or Life in the Woods* (Boston: Ticknor and Fields, 1854). Many excellent online versions of this classic text are available.

[24] Susannah's Wesley's "Rules for Raising Children" is available through many different sources.

Endnotes

[25] This is a well-known news story, but perhaps the most poignant retelling comes from Ashley Smith herself, in a transcript available at http://www.cnn.com/2005/LAW/03/14/smith.transcript/

[26] Morris, Leon. The Gospel According to St. Luke: An Introduction and Commentary. In Tyndale New Testament Commentaries. (Grand Rapids: William B. Eerdmans Publishing Company, 1974), 338-339.

[27] Henley, Larry, and Silbar, Jeff Alan. *Wind Beneath My Wings* (LosAngeles, CA: WB Gold Music Corp, 1982)